III
MUNICIPAL GOVERNMENT

STUDIES IN HISTORY, ECONOMICS AND PUBLIC LAW

EDITED BY

THE UNIVERSITY FACULTY OF POLITICAL SCIENCE

OF COLUMBIA COLLEGE.

Volume V]   _____   [Number 3

MUNICIPAL GOVERNMENT

IN

MICHIGAN AND OHIO:

A STUDY IN THE RELATIONS OF CITY AND COMMONWEALTH

BY

DELOS F. WILCOX

AMS PRESS
NEW YORK

COLUMBIA UNIVERSITY
STUDIES IN THE
SOCIAL SCIENCES

15

The Series was formerly known as *Studies in History,
Economics and Public Law.*

Reprinted with the permission of Columbia University Press
From the edition of 1896, New York
First AMS EDITION published 1968
Manufactured in the United States of America

Library of Congress Catalogue Card Number: 68-56697

AMS PRESS, INC.
New York, N.Y. 10003

TABLE OF CONTENTS.

CHAPTER I.

INTRODUCTORY.

CHAPTER II.

CONSTITUTIONAL PROVISIONS FOR CITIES IN MICHIGAN.

(v)

vi

CONTENTS.

CHAPTER V.

MUNICIPAL LEGISLATION IN OHIO UNDER THE CONSTITUTIONAL LIMITATIONS
OF 1851.

CHAPTER VII.

The Development of Cleveland's Charter.

CHAPTER VIII.

Detroit and Cleveland; a Review of their Municipal Experience.

CHAPTER IX.

The Elements of a City Charter.

CHAPTER X.

The City and the Commonwealth.

CHAPTER I.

I. *Necessity of studying the legal relations of cities.*

DURING the last few decades city life in the United States has been vastly expanded, and consequently the importance of city governmental functions has been multiplied many times. This one fact would be sufficient to justify a careful study of the legal foundations of the city in our polity. The great blunders in our municipal administration, and the numerous and formidable attempts of recent years to reform and recreate our city governmental organizations, make such a study an absolute necessity. In order that improvement may come in government or business, the first thing needful is to know the precise existing condition of affairs, and the leading causes that have operated to bring it about. Reformers too often forget that no matter what ideal state we are coming *to*, we must get there *from* our present position.

It is not necessary to discuss in this study how large a sphere government should take to itself in dealing with great aggregations of people. But however much it does undertake, that much it ought certainly to perform, and perform in the best possible way. City misgovernment is not a new thing, born in the last decade of the nineteenth century. For some reason, which every one would be glad to understand thoroughly, we have had bad government ever since we have had large cities. An immense amount of moral energy has been spent in reformatory efforts, but much of it has apparently gone to waste through ignorance and hasty anger. As in all movements for reform, these efforts have taken one of two directions. They have tried either to get new and better laws, or to bring about a better enforcement and administration of existing laws. A good deal of time is wasted in discussing which of these two methods should be adopted, for we must recognize that the fundamental force in every real advancement is the pressure all along the line. The brunt of the battle for the triumph of conscience, loyalty to the highest ideals, which is at the basis of all good citizenship, must be borne by religion and ethics. The student of political science has for his task to find the ways and means of putting into execution the dictates of the public conscience. One of the most important parts of his task is to discover the general methods of legislation and the general forms of law which are most conducive to economical and effective administration.

II. *Evils of special legislation.*

By the middle of this century the evils of local and special legislation by the central legislative bodies of the states had already become quite alarming. These special laws were occupied chiefly with the chartering and regulating of single corporations, municipal as well as private. There were two distinct evils involved in this system. First, the statute-books became loaded with an enormous mass of purely local regulations, which did not interest the people as a whole, while a great deal of the legislature's time was taken up in their passage. The results were long legislative sessions, partial neglect of general interests and increased expense. Second, laws were passed for individual localities with no sufficient guarantees that the people of the localities wanted or needed such laws. Each locality had one or more representatives in the legislature, and they practically decided what local bills should pass. Thus no deliberation and no publicity were assured, and very often measures were passed on petition of comparatively few citizens of the place affected. For the theory of special legislation was to give each locality what it

wanted; and the only means of knowing that, was through
petitions and the will of the locally chosen members of the
legislature. From these two evils, inherent in the system,
there followed two other evils of a political nature. The ordinary right to dictate local legislation became a subject of
barter, and what is popularly known as "log-rolling" became
a common method of forcing through special bills. On the
other hand, the right formally reserved to the general legislature of passing upon local bills, became a dangerous thing
when the political complexion of the legislature happened to
differ from that of any particular locality of importance. For
the temptation was strong, and many times irresistible, for the
party having power in the central government to interfere
directly with local matters, and exploit the local administration for partisan purposes. Thus we see that in unrestricted
special legislation there were two evils, one inherent and one
resultant, from the standpoint of the state at large, and also
from the standpoint of the city. On the one side the mere
bulk of legislation caused expense, and its character fostered
unsavory legislative methods. On the other side, legislation
by the central authorities destroyed municipal responsibility,
and ended in state interference in purely local affairs.

III. *Constitutional remedies.*

The attempt was made to cure these evils by constitutional
restrictions on the local legislative powers of the state legislatures. The usual remedy tried was the absolute prohibition of
special legislation for cities. But New York, Michigan and Wisconsin, with their strong spirit of local self-government embodied in the deliberative town-meeting and the supervisor system
of county government, took a different course. Before any
state had attempted to forbid special legislation for cities, these
three had put into their constitutional law a guarantee of local
autonomy in the provision assuring to localities the choice of
local officers, thus forestalling to some extent the secondary

evil of special legislation which afterwards became so promi-
nent in many states, namely, the interference of the legislature
for partisan purposes in the appointment of local officers.[1]
Virginia also adopted a similar provision in 1851.[2] In 1851
Ohio and Indiana inaugurated the attempt to forbid special
municipal legislation by constitutional provisions.[3] These two
states had no deliberative town-meeting, or supervisor system,
and although the spirit of local self-government was strong,
still they received their institutions and population more largely
from Pennsylvania and the South than from New York and
New England. It was natural, therefore, that these two commonwealths should be more impressed with the dangers of
special legislation to the state as a whole, involved in long
sessions of the legislature, big volumes of session laws, and
" log-rolling." Two other states, Iowa[4] and Kansas,[5] adopted
this method of constitutional restriction before the War.
Since then the following states have taken similar action in the
years mentioned : Florida,[6] 1865 ; Nebraska,[7] 1867; Arkansas,[8] 1868 ; Illinois,[9] 1870 ; West Virginia, 1872[10] ; Texas[11] and
Pennsylvania,[12] 1873 ; New Jersey[13] and Missouri,[14] 1875 ; Cali-

[1] N. Y. Constitution of 1846, art. vi, sec. 18, art. x, sec. 2 ; Wisc. Cons. of 1848,
art. xiii, sec. 9 ; Mich. Cons. of 1850, art. xv, sec. 14, interpreted in *The People vs.
Hurlbut*, 24 Mich., 44.

[2] Va. Cons. of 1851. art. vi, sec. 34.

[3] Ohio Cons. of 1851, art. xiii, secs. 1 and 6 ; Indiana Coni. 1851, of art. x, sec.
14, and schedule, paragraph 5.

[4] Iowa Cons. of 1857, art. iii, sec 30, art. viii, sec. 1.

[5] Kansas Cons. of 1859, art. xii, secs. 1 and 5.

[6] Florida Cons. of 1865, art. iv, sec. 20.

[7] Nebraska Cons. of 1867, art. on corporations, secs. 1 and 4.

[8] Arkansas Cons. of 1868, art. v, secs. 48 and 49.

[9] Illinois Cons. of 1870, art. iv, sec. 20.

[10] West Virginia Cons. of 1872, art. vi, sec. 39.

[11] Texas Cons., amendment of 1873, art. xii, sec. 40.

[12] Pennsylvania Cons. of 1873, art. iii, sec. 7.

[13] New Jersey Cons., amendments of 1875, art. iv, sec. 7, paragraphs 9 and 11.

[14] Missouri Cons. of 1875, art. iv, sec. 53, art. ix, sec. 70.

fornia[1] and Louisiana,[2] 1879; North Dakota,[3] South Dakota,[4] Wyoming[5] and Washington,[6] 1889; Mississippi,[7] 1890; Kentucky,[8] Minnesota[9] and Wisconsin,[10] 1892. Of these states, Texas in 1876 made the prohibition applicable only to cities with less than 10,000 inhabitants,[11] and Florida, after having embodied it in two constitutions, omitted it from the last one adopted in 1887.[12] In the Louisiana constitution New Orleans was specially excepted from the provision. Missouri, California and Washington at the same time that they forbade special municipal legislation, granted to all cities above a fixed population the right to frame their own charters.[13] Other

[1] California Cons. of 1879, art. xi, sec. 6.

[2] Louisiana Cons. of 1879, art. 46.

[3] North Dakota Cons. of 1889, art. ii, sec. 69, art. vi, sec. 130.

[4] South Dakota Cons. of 1889, art. iii, sec. 23, art. x, sec. 1.

[5] Wyoming Cons. of 1889, art. iii, sec. 27, art. xiii, sec. 1.

[6] Washington Cons. of 1889, art. ii, sec. 26, art. xi, sec. 10.

[7] Mississippi Cons. of 1890, art. vii, sec. 178.

[8] Kentucky Cons. of 1892, secs. 59 and 156.

[9] Minnesota Cons., amendment of 1892, art. iv, sec. 33.

[10] Wisconsin Cons., amendment of 1892, art. iv, sec. 31.

[11] Texas Cons. of 1876, art. iii, sec. 56, art. xi, secs. 4 and 5.

[12] Florida Cons. of 1868, art. v, secs. 17, 18, 21 and 22; Cons. of 1887, art. iii, sec. 24, art. viii, sec. 8. Sections 21 and 24 of article iii are interesting:

Sec. 21. Special or local acts may be passed, "Provided that no local or special bill shall be passed unless notice of the intention to apply therefor shall have been published in the locality where the matter or thing to be affected may be situated, which notice shall state the substance of the contemplated law, and shall be published at least sixty days prior to the introduction into the legislature of such bill, and in the manner to be provided by law. The evidence that such notice has been published shall be established in the legislature before such bill shall be passed."

Sec. 24. "The legislature shall establish a uniform system of county and municipal government, which shall be applicable, except in cases where local or special laws are provided by the legislature that may be inconsistent therewith."

[13] Missouri Cons. of 1875, art. ix, secs. 16, 17, 24 and 25; California Cons. of 1879, art. xi, sec. 8, and amendments of 1887 and 1890; Washington Cons. of 1889, art. xi, sec. 10. For an interesting and careful account of these provisions and their working, see Oberholzer, *Home Rule for American Cities*, Annals of the American Academy of Political and Social Science, vol. 3, pp. 736–763.

states have adopted other constitutional provisions for the government of cities, most of them aimed more or less definitely at the evils of special legislation.[1] We should naturally expect that these evils would be attacked in different states from different points of view, varying with the character of local institutions, the constitutional frame of mind of the people, the peculiar development of the evils to be remedied, and the opportunity for taking advantage of the experience of other states.

IV. *Geographical distribution of constitutional limitations upon special legislation, and their relation to local institutions.*

If we glance at a map of the United States with a table of the constitutional provisions of the commonwealths with reference to local and special legislation before us, we shall notice that those commonwealths which have tried to prevent special acts in reference to municipal government, comprise a belt through the central part of the country running without a break from New Jersey to Wyoming, and stretching up and down the Mississippi Valley. California and Washington, on the Pacific slope, and Florida, lie entirely outside of this belt. If we omit Florida, which has gone back to special legislation, the two states beyond the Rockies are the only ones not included in this belt. It is true that there is little in the way of history, institutional development or location common to this group of states as it now stands. But if we look at the dates when constitutional prohibitions of special legislation were adopted, we see that the movement began in Ohio and Indiana, and that its extension to the extreme northward and the extreme southward is a comparatively recent development. Not till 1879 did Louisiana join the list, and Mississippi and Kentucky followed in 1890 and 1892. On the other side, the

[1] For more detailed facts and references, as well as for the discussion of this general question, see Prof. Goodnow's chapter on "Constitutional Limitations," in *Municipal Home Rule*, pp. 56–98.

Dakotas formed their constitutions as late as 1889, and Minnesota and Wisconsin adopted constitutional amendments forbidding special legislation in 1892. It is apparent that this movement has had a peculiarly strong impulse in those commonwealths which stretch off to the west from Pennsylvania.

There are three well-recognized types of local organization in the United States. New England has developed the town system, while the south has developed the county system. In the middle and western states we find the mixed or township-county system, which is itself differentiated into the New York and Pennsylvania systems. In the New York plan there is a deliberative town-meeting and a board of supervisors representing the townships in the county government. In the Pennsylvania plan there is no deliberative town-meeting, and the county is governed by a board of commissioners, not representatives of the several townships. Of course, New England is the home of the strongest development of local autonomy, but the deliberative town-meeting in a more or less attenuated form is found also in New Jersey, New York, Michigan, Wisconsin, Minnesota and South Dakota, and in parts of Illinois, Nebraska, and North Dakota. Illinois began with the county system in 1818, but introduced the county-option plan by the constitution of 1848, under which most of the counties have organized on the New York plan. A similar option provision was introduced into the Nebraska constitution of 1875, under which a much smaller proportion of counties have organized townships. The Pennsylvania plan is prevalent in Pennsylvania, Ohio, Indiana, Iowa, Kansas and Missouri, while the county system in one form or another has spread over all or most of the remaining states.[1]

It is not strange that the strength of local institutions should have a marked effect on the constitutional methods of

[1] For an extended account of the various systems of local government in the Commonwealths, see Prof. Howard's book, *An Introduction to the Local Cons. Hist. of the U. S.*

dealing with city legislation. If it be true, as a perusal of the convention debates and the generally recognized way of passing most local bills would seem to indicate, that special legislation for municipalities originally was a part of the theory of local autonomy, and only after the growth of large cities came to be used for purposes of central interference, we should expect those states where the idea of local self-government is most strongly developed to be slow about prohibiting special legislation. Looking over the dates again, it is seen that of the states with a uniform deliberative town-meeting system, New Jersey, in 1875, was the first to prohibit special legislation. Not till 1889 and 1892 did South Dakota, Minnesota and Wisconsin do likewise. The adoption of a political experiment in any of the American states is likely to be imitated in others, where there is a like need. It is very probable that New Jersey was influenced by the action taken by Pennsylvania in 1873. In like manner the Dakotas, Minnesota and Wisconsin were undoubtedly influenced by the action of the many states which had adopted the provision prior to 1889. It may also be true that the great proportion of German and Scandinavian inhabitants in the latter two states facilitated the change. I do not know how much the old-world experience of these classes of the population in methods of city government by general laws may have directly influenced their attitude in this country, but they certainly would be more free from the ingrained prejudices and traditions of the New England town-meeting system, than natives of the northern states of the Union are. In considering the connection between the idea of local self-government and special legislation in these states, it must also be remembered that the town-meeting of the west is only a faint copy of its new England prototype, while the growth of cities and the city problem followed much more closely upon the settlement of the country in the west than in the east. It is also an important consideration that special legislation in recent years has tended more and more to take the form of central interference in local affairs.

On the other hand, we find that by 1875 all the states whose local government was organized on the Pennsylvania plan had prohibited special legislation for cities. The same course had been followed by a few states with the county system, as well as by Illinois, which had a combination of the New York and the county systems. Uniformity and centralization naturally go together. And so it is not strange that the states having the more centralized local administrations in the shape of the county and the Pennsylvania systems, should be in a better frame of mind for requiring uniform municipal legislation.

If now we look at the attempts made to guarantee local autonomy in the choice of municipal officers, we see that New York, Michigan and Wisconsin, which form a group by themselves in matters of local organization, all put cities and villages on the same general basis as townships and counties, as far as the choice of officers was concerned. Illinois with its mixed system not only prohibited special legislation, but also adopted a provision authorizing the legislature to delegate the power of local taxation to the corporate authorities of the local divisions.[1] By the interpretation of the Supreme Court this provision was given practically the same force in regard to the local choice of local officers, as was given to the more specific provisions in the three other states.[2] It may be supposed that Virginia, which adopted a provision similar to these in 1851, was influenced by the example of New York. At any rate the supposition is natural, when we consider that Jefferson was an ardent admirer of the New England town-meeting, and the constitutional changes in the state during the first half of this century were along the line of introducing local election districts and elective officers.[3]

We must not over-emphasize the influence of the local sys-

[1] Illinois Cons. of 1848, art. ix, sec. 5 ; Cons. of 1870, art. ix, secs. 9 and 10.

[2] Harward *v.* The St. Clair and Monroe Levee and Drainage Co., 51 Ill., 130, and People *v.* The Mayor, etc., of Chicago, 51 Ill., 17.

[3] Howard, *op. cit.*, pp. 231, 464.

tems of government existing in the several states in determining their respective methods of dealing with the evils of special
legislation for cities. For the spirit of local self-government
is strong in all the states, and the populations and institutions
of all the newer states are a great deal mixed. This much is
certain however, that the two most important attempts to solve
the city problem in constitutional law have been inaugurated
by states having the township-county system; the prohibition
of special legislation having its origin in states with the Pennsylvania type, and the guarantee of the localities against central interference in the choice of their officers having its origin
in states with the New York type.[1] These two methods are
radically different; the one approaching the evils from the
standpoint of the central governments and attempting to protect them from the burden of local and special law-making,
the other approaching the evils from the standpoint of the
localities and attempting to protect them from the interference
of the central authorities in local affairs. Here we have the
most important antithesis in the methods and motives of placing the city within the domain of constitutional law.

V. *Michigan and Ohio as typical States.*

The bulk of migration from the eastern states to the western
has moved along nearly parallel lines, but the farther west

---

[1] This fact is interesting in connection with Prof. Howard's statement, page 135,
that " the western township-county plan is the most advanced phase of local institutions." In reference to the New York system, he says on page 158: " In short,
the representative township-county system of the northwest seems to be one of
the most perfect products of the English mind, and worthy to become, as it not
improbably may become, the prevailing type in the United States." It will be interesting to notice the comparative success of the two methods of establishing the
status of the city in constitutional law, emanating from the Pennsylvania and the
New York systems of local institutions. It should be remarked also, as bearing on
Prof. Howard's second statement, that New York in its last constitution, 1894, has
gone beyond all other states in its efforts to provide a further solution for the problems of city government. New England, with its extreme local spirit, has done
practically nothing to establish the status of the city in constitutional law.

the streams of population have gone, the more they have
mingled. The tendency has been for the men from the eastern
states to carry their institutions with them. In view of these
facts, I believe that Michigan and Ohio offer as good a field
for the study of the constitutional phase of the city problem
as any two states in the Union. On the one hand, they are
free from the conservatism which we think of as attaching to
the "old thirteen;" while on the other hand, they are not
far enough west to prevent a marked differentiation in their
population elements. Ohio is almost a daughter of Pennsylvania, as Michigan is of New York.[1] And besides, Michigan
and Ohio are old enough to have had experience with the
municipal problem, while that experience has not been dis-
torted by the all-commanding presence of some one great
metropolis like New York city, Philadelphia, or Chicago.
Ohio is a good representative of the Pennsylvania plan of local
institutions, and was one of the first two states to prohibit
special legislation. And this constitutional provision has certainly been interpreted and evaded in as remarkable a manner
in Ohio as in any other state. Michigan on the other hand is
a good representative of the New York system of local organ-

---

[1] In the Michigan Constitutional Convention of 1850, which framed the present
constitution of the state, the nativities of the 100 members were as follows : New
England, 38; New York, 43 ; New Jersey, 2 ; Pennsylvania, 3 ; Ohio, 2 ; Michigan, Virginia and North Carolina, each 1 ; foreign countries, 9. Of the native
American population born outside of the state, by the census of 1850, New York
alone had furnished more than 66 % per cent., which added to the contributions
of New England and New Jersey, made a total of 85 % from town-meeting
states. Pennsylvania and Ohio furnished 13 %, while less than two per cent. came
from the southern states.

In the Ohio Constitutional Convention of 1851, which also framed the present
state constitution, the nativities of the 115 members were as follows : Ohio, 31 ;
New England, 21 ; New York, 10; Pennsylvania, 27 ; Delaware, 2 ; Maryland,
4; Virginia, 8 ; Kentucky, 3 ; New Jersey, District of Columbia, and Tennessee,
each 1 ; foreign countries, 5. Of the native American population born outside of the
state, by the census of 1850, Pennsylvania alone had furnished 37 %, while all the
town-meeting states together had furnished a little less than 33 % per cent. More
than 28 % had come from southern states.

ization, and adopted the constitutional guarantee of local choice of municipal officers just a year before Ohio took the other course. The experience of Michigan is of particular value also because of the extreme development by its courts of the idea of local self-government as a doctrine of American constitutional law.

VI. *Detroit and Cleveland as typical American cities.*

In order that we may study intelligently the relations of the municipality and the commonwealth in any particular state, it is needful to take up somewhat in detail the charter history of at least one typical city in that state. Only in this way can we see the practical workings of constitutional theories. Almost everywhere, in Europe as well as in America, the very large cities are less typical of the systems of municipal government than are cities of the second grade. For many reasons the study of the government of Paris, London, New York and Chicago throws less light on the general forms and conditions of city government than the study of smaller cities. The metropolis is really an exception in matters of municipal government, partly because such a city overshadows the provincial towns by its population and wealth, and partly because in the old world the metropolis is the seat of the national government. In America, where municipal government derives its forms and functions from the several commonwealths, the tendency of a city like New York or Chicago to eclipse other cities is greater than in Europe. At the same time the delegation of the most important political functions to the Federal government, makes the adminstration of a great metropolis a much larger affair in proportion to the total sphere of state government than it is in a completely nationalized system. And further, the presence in our great cities of such large masses of foreigners, coming from all parts of Europe, and as yet unassimilated by the native population on account of the recent and quick development of these cities, has helped to make American legislatures very distrustful of the political capacity of the population of the largest cities. It has, therefore, been the rule with us that the larger the number of people living in one place, and the greater and more varied their needs, the less they should be allowed to care for themselves.[1]

Of the American cities of the second grade, Cleveland and Detroit are good examples.[2] Here the interference of the central state authorities in local affairs has never reached the degree attained in New York, for instance, but the problems of city government have nevertheless claimed enough attention to bring about much special legislation and some violation of the principle of local self-government. As American cities go, Detroit and Cleveland have been fairly well governed. At the same time they have been free from the traditions of colonial charters, and yet have had longer experience than cities like San Francisco and Minneapolis. They are distinctively American cities, belonging fully to the national period, and open to all the tendencies peculiar to our political system making for or against good city government. It is significant also that Detroit, under the Michigan idea of local self-government, has in recent years entered upon a period of civic development which promises to put the " city of the straits " in the front rank of self-governing cities in the course of time. On the other hand, Cleveland under Ohio's nominal system of general legislation, has within the last few years secured a plan of government almost unequaled among American cities in its unity and centralization.

[1] This is perhaps equally true of European cities, notably Paris. But in their case, this attitude of the central government is largely influenced by the consideration of the political influence of the great cities as being national capitals. It might be safe to say that this political reason in Europe has about as much weight as the distrust of foreign-born citizens has in this country.

[2] Population, 1890 : Cleveland, 261,353 ; Detroit, 205,876.

VII. *Outline of the plan of study*

Having chosen Michigan and Ohio as typical states, and Detroit and Cleveland as typical cities, for the study of American municipal government in its constitutional relations, I will devote the following chapters to a somewhat detailed consideration of the course of development of the relations between city and commonwealth in the two states. First, the adoption of constitutional provisions and the debates of conventions in Michigan will be discussed. Then the chapter on the doctrine of local self-government in Michigan will show the interpretation given to the constitutional provisions by the Supreme Court. In like manner two chapters on Ohio will deal with the adoption of constitutional provisions and their interpretation by the legislature and the Supreme Court. After this a chapter each will be devoted to the charters of Detroit and Cleveland, and another chapter will present a review and summary of the main features of their governmental experience. The last two chapters will be more theoretical, presenting a few general conclusions in regard to the elements of a city charter and the relation of the city to the state.

CHAPTER II.

MICHIGAN was admitted to the Union as a state in 1837, under a constitution adopted for that purpose two years earlier. In those times municipal corporations had as yet attained constitutional recognition in very few of the states. The only restriction imposed by the first Michigan constitution on the discretion of the legislature in providing for the government of cities and towns was the general provision that no act of incorporation should be passed without the assent of at least two-thirds of each house of the legislature.[1]

I. *The Convention of 1850, and its work.*

In the years preceding 1850 Michigan was not exempt from the general corporation craze, and the reactionary distrust that caused so many constitutional prohibitions of special incorporation acts. At the same time there seems to have been a steady growth in the popular faith in local self-government. This led to a careful distinction in the constitution of 1850 between private and municipal corporations.[2] The question of prohibiting special legislation for cities seems not to have been seriously debated in the convention. It is true, a motion was made to introduce this section, " It shall be the duty of the legislature to provide by general laws for the organization and regulation of cities and villages."[3] But the proposition was voted down almost at once after a delegate "asked if gentle-

---

[1] Constitution of 1835, art. xii, sec. 2.

[2] Constitution of 1850, art. xv, secs. 1, 8 and 10.

[3] Convention Debates, 1850, p. 595.

men really thought it possible to make a general law applicable to all the particular cases that must necessarily arise..
The wisdom of Minerva and of the gentleman from Kent combined could not do it."[1]   The most important action taken by
the convention was in regard to the right of local autonomy.
The following provisions were adopted by the convention and
are the constitutional law of the municipalities of the state
to-day :

(1) " The legislature may confer upon organized townships,
incorporated cities and villages, and upon the board of supervisors of the several counties, such powers of a local, legislative and administrative character as they may deem proper."[2]

(2) " Municipal courts of civil and criminal jurisdiction may
be established by the legislature in cities."[3]

(3) " The legislature shall provide for the incorporation and
organization of cities, and villages, and shall restrict their
powers of taxation, borrowing money, contracting debts, and
loaning their credit." [4]

(4) " Judicial officers of cities and villages shall be elected
and all other officers shall be elected or appointed at such
time and in such manner as the legislature may direct." [5]

(5) " Private property shall not be taken for public improvements in cities or villages without the consent of the owner,.
unless the compensation therefor shall first be determined by
a jury of freeholders, and actually paid or secured in the manner provided by law." [6]

(6) " Previous notice of any application for an alteration of
the charter of any corporation shall be given in such manner
as may be provided by law." [7]

The most important, perhaps, of these provisions, was the

---

[1] Convention Debates, 1850, p. 596.

[2] Constitution of Mich., art. iv, sec. 38.   [3] *Ibid.*, art. vi, sec. 1.

[4] *Ibid.*, art. xv, sec. 13.   [5] *Ibid.*, art. xv, sec. 14.

[6] *Ibid.*, art. xv, sec. 15.   [7] *Ibid.*, art. xv, sec. 16.

fourth.   As first adopted by the convention and referred to the
" Committee on Phraseology and Arrangement," it read thus :
" All judicial officers of cities and villages shall be elected at
such time and in such manner as the legislature may direct.
All other officers of such cities and villages shall be elected
by the electors thereof, or appointed by such authorities
thereof as the legislature shall designate for that purpose." [1]
The committee reported it back to the convention in much
briefer form : " Officers of cities and villages shall be elected
at such times and in such manner as the legislature may
direct." [2]   On motion of Mr. McClelland, of Detroit, it was
amended to its present form.   It was the particular desire of
the convention to guarantee the popular election of all judicial
officers, for they had been the last to yield to the growing
tide of democratic feeling.   It was also seen that some municipal officers might be better appointed than elected, and for
the sake of brevity the manner of their appointment was left
simply to the discretion of the legislature.   The first provision
also, which gave the legislature authority to delegate local
legislative and administrative powers, was important.   It
seems to have been intended to encourage the granting of
large privileges of local autonomy, which some thought the
legislature was hardly authorized to provide for in the absence
of special constitutional provisions.

II. *The Convention of 1867.*

Another convention met in 1867, and adopted a constitution
which the people rejected.   Its provisions and the debates
over them are valuable, however, as furnishing an index of the
growth in importance of the city problem, and as showing the
remedies that suggested themselves to the constitution-makers
of thirty years ago.   In the early days of the convention a
resolution was introduced to the effect, " That the committee

---

[1] Convention Debates, 1850, p. 594.   [2] *Ibid.*, p. 904.

on organization and government of cities and villages be instructed to inquire into the expediency of requiring the legislature to provide for the organization of cities and villages, by general laws, and prohibiting amendments thereof of a merely local character."[1]   Later, when the article on the Legislative Department was being considered, it was moved to add to the section authorizing the grant of powers to local bodies, copied from the constitution of 1850, the words: "The legislature shall provide by general laws for organizing townships, cities and villages, on such conditions and subject to such regulations as may be prescribed. No special acts to create any such organization, or defining their powers, except cities containing over 10,000 inhabitants, shall hereafter be passed by the legislature."[2]   In the discussion of this proposition many objections were raised to any cast-iron rule, because of the diversity of needs in various cities and villages. The delegate who had introduced the resolution quoted above, interpreted the plan now under discussion as meaning that the legislature could make a skeleton of law, to be filled in by the particular localities, according to their needs. In the objections raised against the measure, the American idea of enumerated powers comes out very strongly, in the assumption that a general law could not enumerate all the provisions required by all the localities. The second part of the proposition was voted down, thirty-one to twenty-one.

In the consideration of the article on cities and villages, taken up in committee of the whole later, the chief debate on municipal matters took place. The first question arose on a motion to put " restrict " in place of " regulate " in the section requiring the legislature to regulate the financial powers of cities and villages.[3]   It was argued that " regulate " gave the legislature a more extended power over the internal affairs of

---

[1] Convention Debates, 1867, vol. i. p. 76.   [2] *Ibid.*, vol. ii, p. 95.

[3] *Ibid.*, vol. ii, p. 296.

the corporation.   It was also argued that such a result was
just what ought not to be.   Although the substitution was
lost in committee, it was afterwards carried in the convention.[1]
The question of special legislation was again introduced by a
delegate from Bay county, in a motion to insert the words
" by general law" in the section requiring the legislature to
provide for the organization of cities and villages.[2]   The mover
said in debate: " The gentleman says it takes but very little
time for the passage of these laws; yet, he admits that when
you come to publish them at last, two-thirds of the volumes of
our session laws consist of legislation of this kind.   Why is
this?   Because some one person interested in this matter sits
down, writes out a charter, sends it to a member of the legislature, who presents it, and it is referred to the committee on
corporations.   That committee do not read it or examine it;
they ask the member who presents it, if it is all right?   If he
says it is, they then report it, and recommend its passage;
nobody reads it, it passes and goes to the Governor for his
approval, and very likely he never reads it; if he does he is a
very persevering man. . . . There are few members of the
legislature who can understand the necessities and wants of
any particular village.   They do not profess to know about it;
they do not attempt to judge.   If any act of incorporation
which is presented suits the member from that locality, they
do not consult anybody else about it.   The people of the
vicinity are not consulted, and often know nothing about the
charter provided for them until the act is passed, and frequently not till some time afterwards.   There was an act passed
for our city last winter, but I could not get a copy of it until
a week ago; no one could get it except those who prepared
it."[3]   He also spoke of the general incorporation act for villages, passed in 1857,[4] which was optional.   Most villages pre-

[1] Convention Debates, 1867, vol. ii, p. 360.   [2] *Ibid.*, vol. ii, p. 297.

[3] *Ibid.*, vol. ii, pp. 297, 298, July 23.   [4] Mich. Laws, 1857, pp.420–431.

ferred to get special charters, and hence the legislature was
relieved from the necessity of correcting the faults of the general law. But his arguments were of no avail. The motion
received fourteen ayes, and the noes were not counted.

The most prolonged and animated debate occurred, however, in reference to the election and appointment of local
officers. Two years earlier, in 1865, a Republican legislature
had concluded that the Democratic city of Detroit could not
adequately keep the peace within its own borders and prevent
negro riots; and consequently had passed a law putting the
Detroit police under a metropolitan board appointed by the
Governor and Senate.[1] The standing committee reported to
the convention a section in the exact words of the existing
constitution ;—" Judicial officers of cities and villages shall be
elected, and all other officers shall be elected or appointed, at
such time and in such manner as the legislature may direct."
The time had passed when there was any reason for singling
out *judicial* officers for election, and Detroit's recent experience had thrown interest in quite another direction. Hence
the veteran ex-Governor, Mr. McClelland of Detroit, who had
been a member of both previous constitutional conventions,
moved to substitute the following : " Mayors and members of
the common council in cities shall be elected by the electors
thereof at large or in their proper wards or districts, as shall
be provided by law. All other municipal officers, or boards
in whom is vested any portion of municipal authority, shall be
elected as aforesaid or appointed by the mayor and common
council, in such manner as shall be provided by law."[2] This
proposition was amended so as to include presidents and
boards of trustees of villages among the elective officers.
During the debate, Mr. Lothrop, also of Detroit, and since then
minister to Russia under President Cleveland, said : "We are
perfectly persuaded that the government of all large cities

[1] Mich. Laws, 1865, pp. 99–115.

[2] Convention Debates, 1867, vol. ii, p. 298.

must take either the one direction or the other; there must be more power, and sufficient power, vested in the chief executive and in the legislative department of the city, or else the power of popular government must be taken away, and exercised through boards provided for by the legislature. In my judgment this last system is utterly destructive of all popular responsibility and government of cities."[1] These arguments prevailed in committee of the whole House by a vote of twenty-nine against twenty-five.[2]

The Republican majority of the convention evidently thought the Detroit Democrats had scored a point. For when the report of the committee of the whole was taken up for final action, the fight was re-opened by Mr. Miles, chairman of the standing committee on cities and villages, who moved the following substitute: "The mayor and aldermen of cities, and the president and board of trustees of villages, shall be elected; and all other officers shall be elected or appointed at such time and in such manner as the legislature may direct."[3] This called forth the best efforts of the Detroit men. Mr. Lothrop said: "If we must be governed by some other power, I prefer not to be governed by boards. I prefer to be governed by a proconsul, to be responsible to the legislature. I do not want these irresponsible boards, this municipal government parceled out into a little portion here, and a little portion there, and another portion somewhere else, each one running his office irrespective and independent of the others; though their duties from the nature of things are so minutely and indirectly combined, that they must be administered as a whole, if administered effectively at all. . . . My idea of the true democratic system of government for a city, as I have already said, is this: A mayor, as the chief executive officer of the city, and a common council as the legislative power of the city, should be elected directly by the people. They

[1] Convention Debates, 1867, vol. ii, p. 299.   [2] *Ibid.*, vol. ii, p. 300.
[3] *Ibid.*, vol. ii, p. 331.

should be responsible to the people, and then they should be clothed with power to make a good government."[1]   On the other side Mr. Conger, afterwards United States Senator, said: "A city is a mere creature of the law; it has no power, no authority, no right, no privilege, no place in the world, except as the legislature, carrying out the will of the people, shall give it a place and a standing."[2]   The very extreme of the local autonomy doctrine was set forth by Mr. Norris, of Washtenaw.   In his speech he said: "What is the principle which we are debating, and which is at stake in this question? It is the principle of self-government, the great leading, distinctive feature between republican and tyrannical government, all the world over.   It is the principle that all the power that rests in this government which is worth having for one moment, rests in the little municipal communities where you and I live, to be exercised by us free from all unnecessary control, free to be used as it best may."[3]   The debate was continued with much animation and occasional ability for a long time, and at the end, the convention reversed the action of the committee of the whole by fifty-seven votes against twenty-six; and thus refused to give the constitutional guarantee asked by the home-rulers.[4]   In the debates there was a singular lack of perception as to the double functions of the municipality — public and local.   Those in favor of self-government tried to force the issue absolutely between despotism and centralization on the one side, and liberty and local autonomy on the other.   The convention refused to accept the dilemma, and adopted a half-way measure, like good Anglo-Saxons.

III. *The Constitutional Commission of 1873.*

I do not know the causes which led to the defeat of the proposed constitution of 1867 at the polls.   But there was evi-

---

[1] Convention Debates, 1867, vol. ii, p. 333.   [2] *Ibid.*, vol. ii, p. 339.

[3] *Ibid.*, vol. ii, p. 343.   *Ibid.*, vol. ii, p. 360.

dently a strong demand for extensive constitutional amendments; for a new effort was made in that direction in 1873. This time the Legislature authorized the Governor to appoint a Constitutional Commission to consist of two members from each of the nine congressional districts, who should prepare a general revision of the fundamental law to be submitted to the next session of the Legislature for approval before going to the people.[1] A resolution was offered at an early session of the Commission, prohibiting the legislature from passing local or special laws, "incorporating cities or villages, or changing or amending the charter of any city or village."[2] As reported by the committee of the whole, the last clause forbidding charter amendments was omitted.[3] The provisions with reference to municipalities finally adopted by the Commission but never incorporated in the constitution were the following:

(1) "Cities and villages shall hereafter be incorporated only under general laws, in which their powers of taxation, borrowing money and contracting debts, shall be restricted."[4]

(2) The limit of indebtedness, including school debts, was placed at ten per cent. of the valuation on the assessment roll.[5]

(3) "The executive and legislative officers of cities and villages shall be elected, and all other officers shall be elected or appointed, at such time and in such manner as the Legislature may direct."[6]

(4) "Existing charters of cities and villages may be altered and amended."[7]

(5) Municipal corporations were forbidden to become stockholders in private enterprises, or lend their credit or make any loan or gift to them, or construct or own any railroad.[8]

[1] Mich. Laws, 1873, Joint Resolution of April 24.
[2] Mich. Cons. Commission, 1873, Journal, pp. 24–26.
[3] *Ibid.*, pp. 35–37.   [4] *Ibid.*, p. 201, art. x, sec. 14.   [5] *Ibid.*, sec. 15.
[6] *Ibid.*, pp. 201–202, art. x, sec. 16.   [7] *Ibid.*, sec. 17.
[8] *Ibid.*, sec. 1, pp. 198–199.

The legislature of 1874 changed the second provision by adding—"unless authorized by a majority of the electors residing within such corporation voting thereon as may be prescribed by law."[1]   The next section was also changed to read thus—"The judicial, chief executive and legislative officers of cities and villages shall be elected."

Although the constitution of 1850 is still Michigan's fundamental law, these various attempts to change it point to the increasing demand that the city should be placed beyond a doubt under the protection of the constitution in some way or other, and at the same time should be held within definite limitations, chiefly financial.

[1] Mich. Laws, 1874, p. 36.

CHAPTER III.

THE courts of Michigan, under the leadership of Judges Cooley, Campbell and Christiancy, have carried the idea of local self-government as a doctrine of American constitutional law farther than, perhaps, any other courts of this country. This fact is interesting here, because it has led to important results in delimiting a sphere of municipal home rule. It is not necessary to go into the details of the early development of local government in Michigan, for that has already been done quite completely.[1] A brief review of the main stages of development will nevertheless be helpful.

I. *Outline of the early development of local self-government.*

By the Ordinance of 1787, the Governor of the Northwest Territory was authorized to divide the territory into counties and townships for administrative and executive purposes, and appoint the local officers.[2] Nine years later the survey was provided for, which formed the basis of the present system of uniform townships, six miles square.[3] The sparseness of population was favorable to the appointment of most officers by the Governor in the early years of the present century. I find no evidence of elective officers within the territory of Michigan prior to 1810, save in Detroit. And even there, under the charter of 1806, the mayor was an appointee of the

---

[1] Bemis, *Local Government in Mich. and the Northwest*, J. H. U. Studies, vol. i, no. 5 ; also, Howard, *Local Const. Hist. of the U. S.*, pp. 153–156, 426–438.

[2] Journals of Congress, vol. iv, pp. 751–754.

[3] U. S. Statutes at Large, vol. i, pp. 464–469.

Governor and was given an absolute veto over the acts of the elective council.[1]   But in 1810 a law was promulgated authorizing the election of five selectmen with very extensive duties in each of the districts of the Territory.[2]   The laws of Governor Hull and the Judges, however, were pretty much paper laws in those days, especially as the war with England soon made a military government a practical necessity.   Under Governor Cass' administration there was a constant development of county and township organization, but for many years the local officers were appointive.   But in 1825 Congress authorized the Governor and Legislative Council to define and incorporate townships whose officers were to be elected. County officers also were to be elected, except that judges and clerks of courts of record, judges of probate, sheriffs and justices of the peace had to be appointed.[3]   Under this act the deliberative town-meeting and the " supervisor system " were introduced in 1827.[4]   By the first state constitution the county and township judicial and peace officers became elective, but the state judiciary continued to be appointive until the second constitution was adopted in 1850.   This early tendency to make an exception of judicial officers in favor of the system of appointment, was doubtless responsible for the wording of the clause adopted in this constitution requiring specifically the election of " judicial officers of cities and villages."   The history of this section in the convention has been told in the preceding chapter.[5]   The powers of the county boards of supervisors were also increased by this constitution.

II. *The doctrine of local self-government developed by the Supreme Court.*

In the year 1853 the legislature made an innovation by establishing a board of water commissioners for Detroit, and

---

[1] Mich. Terr. Laws, vol. iv, pp. 3–6.   [2] *Ibid.*, vol. iv, pp. 96, 97.

[3] U. S. Statutes at Large, vol. iv, pp. 80, 81.

[4] Mich. Terr. Laws, vol. ii, pp. 317–325, 325–329.   [5] *Supra*, p. 27.

naming the first members in the act itself.[1] The first appointees were to hold for one, two, three, four and five years respectively, their successors to be chosen by the common council. This act was not tested in the courts. But eleven years later a law creating a metropolitan board of police commissioners,[2] although the first members were named in the act, and their successors were to be appointed by the Governor and Senate, was upheld in the case of People vs. Mahaney.[3] The effects of this action on the deliberations of the constitutional convention of 1867 have already been noted.[4] The decision of the court in the case of the police commissioners was followed by the enactment of several laws creating boards for the city of Detroit, the first members being named in the acts, though their successors were to be appointed by the corporate authorities. In 1867 a fire commission was appointed by the legislature,[5] and at the session of 1871 the police law was reënacted and the appointments renewed,[6] and boards of park commissioners[7] and public works[8] were appointed. The park board was to consist of six members, one-third to retire each year and their successors to be appointed for three-year terms by the council on nomination of the

[1] Mich. Laws, 1853, pp. 180–187.   [2] Ibid., 1865, pp. 99–115.

[3] 13 Michigan, 481. In this case the question of central appointment of local officers, as affected by art. xv, sec. 14, of the Constitution was not considered. Section 13, which required the legislature to *restrict* the taxing powers of cities, and several other provisions of the constitution in reference to the forms of legislation, were considered. It was also argued by counsel that the act violated the principal of "no taxation without representation." This view was not sustained by the court, which held that Detroit was represented both in the Legislature and in the election of the Governor. Later, in the case of People *v.* Hurlbut, 24 Mich., 44, this decision was cited by counsel for the Board of Public Works, but Chief Justice Campbell distinguished the cases on the ground that the police commissioners were essentially state officers, while the board of public works were entirely local in their functions.

[4] *Supra*, pp. 30–32.   [5] Mich. Laws, 1867, vol. ii, pp. 931–938.

[6] Ibid., 1871. vol. iii, pp. 230–254.

[7] Ibid., 1871, vol. ii, pp. 1322–1334.   [8] Ibid., vol, iii, pp. 278–287.

mayor. The board of public works consisted of four members, two of each political party, one to retire every two years, and their successors to be appointed by the city authorities. The old boards of sewer commissioners and water commissioners were to be superseded by this new board, but they refused to give up their offices, and action was brought against them by *quo warranto* to test the validity of the law.[1] The court decided that the appointment of the board of public works for definite terms by the central authority of the state was unconstitutional.

The opinion in this case was very long, each judge feeling compelled to speak for himself. The provision of the constitution which came nearest to the question at stake was the one requiring the election of judicial officers in cities, and the election or appointment of other officers " at such time and in such manner as the Legislature may direct."[2] The history of this section in the convention of 1850 was an important factor in establishing the intention of the framers with reference to the appointment of local officers. Having referred to the inevitable inference that the *election* of local officers meant election by the *people of the localities,* Judge Christiancy, in delivering the first opinion, went on to say: " The inference that the appointments referred to in this provision were intended to be such only as the legislature might authorize the local authorities to make, may not be so palpable at first view, as there is no provision how appointments in general shall be made ; and all that are authorized of a local character are not required to be made by the local authorities of the district or locality for which the appointment is to be made. But when we recur to the history of the country, and consider the nature of our institutions, and of the government provided for by this constitution, the vital importance which in all the states has been so long attached to local municipal governments by the people

---

[1] People *v.* Hurlbut, 24 Mich., 44.

[2] Constitution of 1850, art. xv, sec. 14.

of such localities, and their rights of self-government, as well
as the general sentiment of hostility to everything in the nature of control by a distant central power in the mere administration of such local affairs, and ask ourselves the question,
whether it was probably the intention of the convention in
framing, or the people in adopting, the constitution, to vest in
the legislature the appointment of all local officers, or to authorize them to vest it elsewhere than in some of the authorities of such municipalities, . . . the conclusion becomes very
strong that nothing of this kind could have been intended by
the provision. And this conviction becomes stronger when we
consider the fact that this constitution went far in advance of
the old one, in giving power to the people which had formerly
been exercised by the executive, and in vesting, or authorizing
the legislature to vest, in municipal organizations a further
power of local organization than had before been given them.
We cannot, therefore, suppose it was intended to deprive cities
and villages of the like benefit of the principle of local self-
government enjoyed by other political divisions of the state."

But this judge considered it proper for the legislature to
appoint persons to organize the board, set it on its feet, and
turn it over to municipal appointees. And for this reason he
considered the act as a whole valid, and favored judgment of
ouster against the hold-over water and sewer commissioners.

Chief Justice Campbell, in his opinion, pointed out that the
decision in the case of People *vs.* Mahaney did not affect the
question here involved, because the police commissioners were
essentially state officers, exercising state functions, while the
board of public works was a confessedly local and municipal
authority. In reference to the other boards appointed by the
legislature heretofore, he argued that the co-operation of the
municipal authorities with them without protest operated as a
ratification of the legislative appointments. But in the present
case there was no such consent. "We are, therefore, compelled to consider the plain question, whether the state author-

ities have the right to assume unlimited control of all
municipal appointments. Judicial offices the constitution has
distinctly provided for as elective; and they are local in their
action rather than in their nature. But as to other offices the
power is plenary, or it does not exist at all. It may as well
include every office as any less than all. It may put all the
power in the hands of one person, as well as divide it among
several, and it may continue it for life as well as for a less
period." Referring to the state constitution, he goes on to
say : "We must never forget, in studying its terms, that most
of them had a settled meaning before its adoption. Instead of
being the source of our laws and liberties, it is, in the main,
no more than a recognition and reënactment of an accepted
system. The rights preserved are ancient rights, and the
municipal bodies recognized in it, and required to be perpetu-
ated, were already existing, with known elements and functions. They were not towns, or counties, or cities or villages
in the abstract—or municipalities which had lost all their old
liberties by central usurpation—but American and Michigan
municipalities of common-law origin, and having no less than
common law franchises. So far as any indication can be found,
in the constitution of 1850, that they were to be changed in
any substantial way, the change indicated is in the direction
of increased freedom of local action, and a decrease in the
power of the state to interfere with local management." The
Chief Justice, after calling attention to the fact that English
and American boroughs have always had the right to choose
their own local officers, and dwelling further on the Michigan
constitutional provisions guaranteeing the local election of
county and township officers, declared that the constitution
could not have intended to give the cities fewer rights. "This
is no mere political theory," he says, "but appears in the constitution as the foundation of all our polity. There is no middle ground. A city has no constitutional safeguards for its
people, or it has the right to have all its officers appointed at

home." He did not even agree that temporary appointments by the legislature for purposes of organization were admissible, and moreover asserted that the bi-partisan clause prescribed unconstitutional tests of opinion for holding public office. Hence the law was void, and judgment of ouster should not be rendered.

Judge Cooley thought the bi-partisan requirement was simply nugatory, agreeing with Judge Christiancy in this respect. The important question with him, as with the others, was the right of self-government involved in the case. The full power of the legislature to create the municipality, enlarge or diminish its powers, or abolish it altogether, was recognized as an accepted doctrine of constitutional law. Judge Cooley added, "But such maxims of government are very seldom true in anything more than a general sense; they never are and never can be literally accepted in practice. Our constitution assumes the existence of counties and townships, and evidently contemplates that the state shall continue to be divided as it has hitherto been; but it nowhere expressly provides that every portion of the state shall have county or township organizations. . . . If, therefore, no restraints are imposed upon legislative discretion beyond those specifically stated, the township and county government of any portion of the state might be abolished, and the people be subjected to the rule of commissions appointed at the capital. . . . The doctrine that within any general grant of legislative power by the constitution there can be found authority thus to take from the people the management of their local concerns, and the choice, directly or indirectly, of their local officers, if practically asserted, would be somewhat startling to our people, and would be likely to lead hereafter to a more careful scrutiny of the charters of government framed by them, lest some time, by an inadvertent use of words, they might be found to have conferred upon some agency of their own, the legal authority to take away their liberties altogether." The origin of local self-

government in the American colonies is reviewed, and an elo-
quent discussion of the meaning of constitutional freedom is
presented.   Referring to the motives of the framers of our institutions, the judge says: "With them it has been an axiom
that our system was one of checks and balances; that each
department of the government was a check upon the others,
and each grade of government upon the rest; and they have
never questioned or doubted that the corporators in each
municipality were exercising their franchises under the protection of certain fundamental principles which no power in
the state could override or disregard.   The state may mould
local institutions according to its views of policy or expediency; but local government is matter of absolute right, and
the state cannot take it away.   It would be the baldest mockery to speak of the city as possessing municipal liberty where
the state not only shaped its government, but at discretion
sent in its own agents to administer it ; or to call that system
one of constitutional freedom under which it should be equally
admissible to allow the people full control in their local affairs,
or no control at all."   But so far as the present case is concerned, local autonomy is clearly enough recognized in the
constitution.   The Judge's words are: "When, therefore, we
seek to gather the meaning of the constitution from ' the four
corners of the instrument,' it is impossible to conclude that the
appointments here prescribed, in immediate connection with
election by the local voters, and by a convention intent on
localizing and popularizing authority, were meant to be made
at the discretion of the central authority, in accordance with
an usage not prevalent since the days of the Stuarts, and which
even then was regarded, both in England and America, as
antagonistic to liberty and subversive of corporate rights."
Nevertheless provisional appointments to put the new system
in operation could be made by the legislature, and hence the
appointees were entitled to their offices for the time being.

The fourth member of the court, Justice Graves, gave only

a short opinion, in which he disputed the authority of the legislature to make even temporary appointments, thus taking a position with the Chief Justice against the other two Justices, and preventing a judgment of ouster. But the court was unanimous, as we have seen, in the opinion that permanent appointments for strictly local offices could be made only by the local authorities. This was the now famous case of People *vs.* Hurlbut, in which the doctrine of an unwritten constitution was proclaimed in Michigan. The legislature could grant, define and restrict local privileges; but whatever powers a municipality might be given, its right to exercise them through its own officers was guaranteed by a law higher than the written instrument adopted in 1850.

In the case of Attorney General *vs.* Lothrop[1] it was soon after held that the Detroit Park Commissioners appointed by the legislature had been in effect confirmed by the common council, when it accepted their plans. Hence they were entitled to hold their offices. Another case involving the question of local acquiescence in the central appointment of officers was that of Hubbard *vs.* The Township Board of Springwells.[2] The legislature had authorized the Governor to appoint three commissioners to take charge of a certain highway within the township, improve it, charge tolls, and require the township to issue bonds and levy taxes to pay the expenses of the improvement.[3] The township board refused to issue the bonds when called upon to do so, and a *mandamus* was applied for to compel them. This the Supreme Court refused on the grounds that the state was prohibited in the constitution from engaging in works of internal improvement, and the act in question violated the rights of local self-government. These commissioners who were to hold in perpetuity and be responsible only to the Governor could in no sense be local officers. But the highway attempted to be put under their authority was already in charge of local authorities provided for in the

[1] 24 Mich., 235.   [2] 25 Mich., 153.   [3] Mich. Laws, 1871, no. 414.

constitution itself.   The court said : "As we held in the case
of the Detroit board of public works, the regulation of the
township affairs, legally concerning none but the people of the
town, cannot be lawfully vested in any officers imposed upon
the township from without.   These commissioners, not appointed by, or responsible to, the township or its people, are
empowered to assume exclusive charge of a town highway,
turn it into a toll-road, and raise money and impose taxes in
the township to complete and repair the work. . . . The
result is that a purely local work, public in its character, is
taken charge of and conducted at local expense, and paid for
by local bonds and taxes, without giving any of the local
authorities any function to perform, except that of yielding
implicit obedience to the orders and requisitions of a commission, in whose appointment and government the town and its
people have had no part whatever."   No amount of inaction
on the part of the township authorities could make the commissioners local officers, because the act provided that they
and their successors should be appointed by the Governor absolutely ; whereas in the case of the Detroit Park Commissioners the appointive power was vested ultimately in the city,
and hence by its acquiescence it could make the legislative
appointees its own.

   But the court was not yet through with the park commission.   The law of 1871, under which the commissioners had
been accepted by the city, conferred upon them purely prelim-
inary and advisory powers, the final determination upon the
purchase of a park being left to the citizens' meeting.   But
Detroit was too large a city to be conducted on the plan of
the New England town, and so two citizens' meetings, called
to decide upon the park question, broke up in confusion, without coming to any agreement.   The next legislature, therefore, abolished the citizens' meeting in Detroit, and explicitly
gave the park commissioners full powers to purchase a park,
and required the common council to issue bonds up to $300,-

000, on the request of the commission.[1]   This the council
refused to do when the time came, and a *mandamus* was applied for to compel them.[2]   The application was refused by
the court on the ground that the state had no right to compel a city to expend money for its purely local concerns, and
the commissioners had not been accepted by the city for the
exercise of the powers conferred upon them by the act of 1873.
In delivering the opinion of the court, Judge Cooley said:
" The proposition that there rests in this or any other court
the authority to compel a municipal body to contract debts
for local purposes against its will, is one so momentous in its
importance, and so pregnant with possible consequences, that
we could not fail to be solicitous when it was presented that
its foundations should be thoroughly canvassed and presented,
and that we might have before us, in passing upon it, all the
considerations that could be urged in its support.   In this our
desire has been gratified to the utmost."   He then made a
clear distinction between matters of general concern enforced
upon the localities, and things of purely local interest in which
the legislature attempts to interfere.   "It is as easy to justify
on principle," he went on to say, "a law which permits the
rest of the community to dictate to an individual what he shall
eat, and what he shall drink, and what he shall wear, as to
show any constitutional basis for one under which the people
of other parts of the state, through their representatives, dictate to the city of Detroit what fountains shall be erected at
its expense for the use of its citizens, or at what cost it shall
purchase, and how it shall improve and embellish a park or
boulevard for the recreation and enjoyment of its citizens."
While he admitted that local functions might be distributed
among the several local authorities by the legislature, yet
some regard must be had to the kind of functions any particu-

[1] Mich. Laws, 1873, vol. ii, pp. 100, 265.

[2] Board of Park Commissioners *v.* Common Council of Detroit, 28 Mich., 228.

lar officer was chosen to perform. The new duties imposed upon the park commission were radically different from the old. Concluding he said, "That government would be a mockery of republican institutions, which while leaving to the people a choice of officers, should afterwards determine whether any particular officer who had been selected by the people should be a legislator or a judge, a governor or a policeman."

The legislature of 1873 again established a board of public works for Detroit, to be locally appointed.[1] The common council refused to act on the nominations of the mayor for the members of this board, but was compelled to do so by *mandamus* granted by the court in the case of Attorney General *vs.* Common Council of Detroit.[2] The objection to this act was based upon the assumption that it essentially changed the form of local government which was universally recognized, by which the council possessed the legislative power of the municipality. Judge Cooley said: "I shall assent to the position of the respondents that the common council of a city—I mean a body commonly known by that name, whether in any particular charter so designated or not—is a distinctive and inseparable feature in municipal government under our existing institutions, and cannot be done away with. . . . I cannot find any safe ground in constitutional law on which the new idea of parceling out the powers of municipal governments among local boards, however chosen, can be supported under the provisions of constitutions adopted when such a system was unknown, and designed to guard and secure a system quite different." Still the main features of the act in question were constitutional, and the powers given to the board of public works might be so interpreted as not to encroach upon the essential legislative sphere of the common council. Hence the council was required to act upon the mayor's nominations, and particular sections of the law might be tested afterwards when the board attempted to exercise doubtful powers.

[1] Mich. Laws, 1873, vol. iii, p. 175.   [2] 29 Mich., 108.

Judge Campbell dissented from the opinion of the court, on the ground that the unconstitutional features of the law formed an integral part of it.

A few years later, at the January term in 1880, the case of *Allor vs. Wayne County Auditors*[1] was decided by the court. Allor was a constable for one of the wards of Detroit, and presented his claim to the county auditors for services in making arrests of persons charged with crimes committed within the county but outside the city of Detroit, the warrants being issued by justices of the peace within the city. The auditors declined to pass upon Allor's claim, on the ground that the metropolitan police act of 1871 conferred upon the police force exclusive power of serving such processes.[2] The court held that constables were officers recognized by the constitution, essentially local peace officers, whose powers could not be taken away by legislative act, or conferred exclusively upon the metropolitan police force, which could be regarded only as a body of state peace officers supplementary to the everywhere existing local peace officers. Judge Campbell again laid down the doctrine of local autonomy. " It is not," said he, "and it certainly cannot be claimed, that under our constitution there can be any such thing as municipal government which is not managed by popular representatives and agencies deriving their authority from the inhabitants. No business which is in its nature municipal can be controlled by state or any other outside authorities." Constables were the only peace officers chosen in Detroit, and were an indispensable part of all municipal government. Hence the provisions of the law in conflict with this fact were invalid, and *mandamus* was granted to compel the auditing of Allor's claim by the county board.

The case of Torrent *vs.* Muskegon[3] was also important in the interpretation of the fundamental powers of a municipality. It seems that the charter of Muskegon gave no power expli-

[1] 43 Mich., 76.   [2] Mich. Laws, 1871, pp. 230–254, secs. 13, 35.
[3] 47 Mich., 115.

citly to construct a city hall, but the council had proceeded to do it nevertheless. Certain taxpayers of the city applied for an injunction. This was refused by the court, and the power to erect a city hall was interpreted as being one of the powers essential in city corporations. The opinion of the court was again delivered by Judge Campbell, who said: "If cities were new inventions, it might with some plausibility be claimed that the terms of their charters, as expressed, must be the literal and precise limits of their powers. But cities and kindred municipalities are the oldest of all existing forms of government, and every city charter must be rationally construed as intended to create a corporation which shall resemble in its essential character the class into which it is introduced. There are many flourishing cities whose charters are short and simple documents. Our verbose charters, except in the limitations they impose upon municipal action, are not as judiciously framed as they might be, and create mischief by their prolixity. But if we should assume that there is nothing left to implication, we should find the longest of them too imperfect to make city action possible." And further, "The constitution of this state . . . contemplates that the Legislature shall create cities and other municipalities, with full powers of beneficial legislation. . . . When the Legislature of the state prescribes the limits of financial action, it must be assumed to permit all reasonable and proper expenditures within those limits."

By an act of 1885, the legislature attempted to establish a bi-partisan "Board of Commissioners of Registration and Election" for Detroit.[1] This board was to be appointed by the mayor and council, and was itself to appoint ward registers and inspectors, equally from the two political parties represented in the council. The council refused to consider the mayor's nominations for the board, and the case came before the Supreme Court in an action for *mandamus* to force the city

[1] Mich. Laws, 1885, p. 281.

367]   *IN MICHIGAN AND OHIO.*   49

fathers to pass upon the names submitted to them.[1]   The writ was denied on three grounds. First, the requirement of equal representation of the two political parties created an unconstitutional "test" for the holding of public office. Second, such important powers of government as those concerning the conduct of elections must be exercised by officers who " derive their powers and office either from the people directly, or from the agents or representatives of the people," and cannot be subdelegated. Third, the provisions of this act interfere with the constitutional right of local self-government. Upon this point it is worth while to quote the following passages: " It is also well settled that our state polity recognizes and perpetuates local government through various classes of municipal bodies whose essential character must be respected, as fixed by usage and recognition when the constitution was adopted. And any legislation for any purpose, which disregards any of the fundamental and essential requisites of such bodies, has always been regarded as invalid and unconstitutional." And further on: " It has always been held in this state that the municipalities which can be created by our Legislature must be such in substantial character as they have been heretofore known. Up to this time, and ever since elections were first held in Michigan, they have been not only localized in some municipal division, but regarded as municipal action and supervised and managed by municipal officers, either directly elected or else appointed by those who have been elected. Such a board as this, which is in no sense a mere agency of the city, is foreign to our system. If it can be created in a city it can just as well be created in a county, or for the State. When the election ceases to be a municipal procedure, the whole foundation of municipal government drops out. And a municipality which is not managed by its own officers is not such a one as our constitution recognizes."

[1] Attorney General *v.* Board of Councilmen of the City of Detroit, 58 Mich., 213.

I have quoted very fully from this series of cases, in order to show in the express words of the court, that the doctrine of local self-government is something more than a theory in Michigan. It is fully recognized that the Legislature may grant, withhold, or take away the corporate powers of cities, but it cannot take away from the people of any locality the fundamental right of managing their own affairs. That is, the essentials of county and township government are guaranteed absolutely to all the people, and if further privileges are given to cities, they can be exercised only by local officers. There are certain general functions, as police, which may be exercised in a supplementary way by state officials, but not to the displacement of ordinary local officers.[1] And further, the Legislature cannot radically change the existing forms of municipal government, as, for instance, by depriving the city council of its essential position as the municipal legislative power.

[1] The Legislature of 1895 reorganized the Detroit Board of Health, giving the appointment of its members into the Governor's hands. This act has not yet been passed upon by the Supreme Court.

CHAPTER IV.

CONSTITUTIONAL PROVISIONS FOR CITIES IN OHIO.

I. *The early development of special legislation.*

By the Constitution of 1802 no provision was made for municipal corporations. But the inhabitants of counties, towns and townships were guaranteed the right to elect their own officers.[1] When we remember that Cincinnati was first incorporated as a city in 1819, it becomes evident that the constitution-makers of 1802 could not have felt the pressure of the problems of city government to any extent. It is not surprising that they were content to leave the work of municipal organization to the legislature. Still the guarantee of local self-government to "towns" was important, as in that term were included embryo city organizations. But the phenomenal growth of Ohio's population during the first half of this century from about 50,000 to almost 2,000,000, and the consequent development of industry, led to the chartering of numberless corporations, including of course many municipalities. The custom of special legislation for the organization of corporations was a natural growth, and not being restricted by constitutional provisions, had become a great evil by the year 1850. At the session of the General Assembly for 1849–50, for instance, 545 local and special acts were passed, 73 of them relating to towns and cities, 78 to turnpike roads, 75 to plank roads, 67 to railway companies, and so on through the list of the various corporate enterprises. At the next session the total number of such acts was 672, making an octavo volume of 709 pages.

---

[1] Constitution of 1802, art. vi, secs. 1 and 3.

II. *The Convention of 1851 and its work.*

The mere bulk of this special legislation would have furnished an urgent reason for the requirement of general incorporation laws. But another force was at work, of greater influence on the public opinion of the state. The over-development of corporate undertakings, and the consequent losses to the community as a whole, were probably the reasons for the intense feeling against corporations that took possession of the popular mind, and called for the constitution of 1851. No better evidence of this can be given than the words of a delegate to the constitutional convention in the debate on the subject. The committee of the whole was discussing a section reported by the committee on the legislative department, providing that " the General Assembly shall provide for the creation and government of municipal corporations by general and uniform laws."[1]   Mr. Leech moved to add, "but no corporate body shall be created, renewed, or extended by special act of the General Assembly." In support of his motion, he said : " Corporations, sir, are destructive to equality, and hostile to free institutions, and their existence should not be tolerated in a republican government. They confer privileges and benefits on the *few*, which are not enjoyed by the *many*. Every special act of incorporation is a grant of monopoly—a charter of privileges to a few individuals, which are not conferred upon the community at large. Such legislation is, consequently, utterly repugnant to the great republican doctrine of equal rights—a doctrine that lies at the basis of the free institutions of this country." Moved by this profound disgust with corporations, the convention made no very careful distinction of public and private corporations. The two standing committees in charge of this general subject were the committee on banking corporations, and the one on "corporations other than banking." In the debate on the proposition to prohibit special

[1] Convention Debates, 1850–51, vol. 1, p. 284.

acts of incorporation, the chairman of the second of these committees, in explaining his report, said that "some of the state
constitutions contained an exception, so far as municipal corporations were concerned.   There was no very definite conclusion come to on the part of the committee, whether this
exception should be named or not; but they concluded however, unanimously, to make this report without a section of
that nature.   They believed that all the corporations of the
state could be as well regulated by general as by special acts
of incorporation—by some classification in cities—by the
number of inhabitants, or by some other manner which might
be thought prudent by the Legislature."[1] Another gentleman argued in favor of the proposition on the ground that acts
of a general nature would get much more careful attention at
the hands of the legislature than special acts.[2]   The latter were
passed almost without interest save on the part of the member
from the locality affected.   Several gentlemen, on the other
hand, argued that special legislation for cities could not be
dispensed with.   It is interesting to note that one of the delegates, a man of German birth, in advocating general laws, said
that he had had some experience with reference to general acts
for cities, and knew the difficulties in the way were not insur-
mountable.[3]   It would simply be necessary to put in the law
general provisions to cover all possible differences of local
needs, and leave it to the individual cities to decide whether
or not to take advantage of them.   This was introducing the
Continental idea of a general grant of corporate power, and
could hardly be expected to appeal in its fullness to Americans, who had come to consider a city charter as much a law as
a grant.   Yet the opinion of those favoring general laws prevailed, and the three following sections were adopted by the
convention and ratified by the people:

[1] Convention Debates, 1850–51, vol. i, p. 340.   [2] *Ibid.*, vol. i, p. 342.

[3] *Ibid.*, vol. i, p. 358.

(1) " The Legislature shall pass no special act conferring corporate powers."[1]

(2) " It shall be the duty of the Legislature to provide for the organization of cities and incorporated villages by general laws, and to restrict their power of taxation, assessment, borrowing money, contracting debts, and loaning their credit, so as to prevent the abuse of such power."[2]

(3) "All laws of a general nature shall have a uniform operation throughout the state."[3]

These provisions are still in force although they have been peculiarly flexible under the practice of the General Assembly and the interpretations of the Supreme Court.

III. *The Convention of 1873–74.*

After twenty years' experience under the constitution of 1851, a convention of the people was called to revise the organic law. It met and debated in the years 1873 and 1874; but the constitution drawn up by it was rejected by the people, and no new constitution has been adopted since. A study of the convention debates of 1873 and 1874 will throw much light, however, upon the sober convictions of the people, always better represented in a constituent than in a legislative assembly. The committee on municipal corporations reported a section as follows:

" The General Assembly shall, by general laws, provide for the organization and classification of municipal corporations; the number of such classes shall not exceed six, and the power of each class shall be defined by general laws, so that no such corporation shall have any other powers or be subject to any other restrictions, than other corporations of the same class. The General Assembly shall restrict the powers of such corporations to levy taxes and assessments, borrow money and contract debts, so as prevent the abuse of such power."[4]

---

[1] Constitution, art. xiii, sec. 1.   [2] *Ibid.*, art. xiii, sec. 6.

[3] *Ibid.*, art. ii, sec. 26.   [4] Ohio Convention Debates, 1873–74, vol. i, p. 578.

Mr. Hoadly of Cincinnati, as chairman of the committee, led off in the debate with a very interesting account of special legislation in Ohio up to date. After citing some of the outrageous and open violations of the constitutional limitations, he said: " The question is whether we will permit the continuance of such legislation or not; and that, I submit, depends upon whether the evils of special legislation are such as to require us still to deny special legislation; for that nearly all of these statutes are unconstitutional and void, as being special legislation, I imagine all lawyers would admit. It is not classification to single out a city having a particular population, or a village of 5,641, and say that any village having that population, as published in that book, *and no more*, shall have authority to build head of division and car shops·"[1] The experience of the past, as well as the inherent elements of the situation, had convinced the enemies of special legislation that some form of classification must be admitted for municipal legislation. It was quite generally agreed that peculiar characteristics of location would always render it desirable to have Cleveland and Cincinnati in different classes. But to put no restriction on the legislative power of classification would only bring about a repetition of the practical nullification of the constitution. Hence the committee, and with them the majority of the convention, determined to fix the maximum number of classes at six, it being generally supposed that each of the two leading cities of the state would be put in a class by itself. The section as adopted, in reality, though not in form, defined a special act as one referring to any less than all of the cities of one class.[2] These provisions were not adopted till after a long debate, conducted with much ability on both sides.

---

[1] Ohio Convention Debates, 1873–74, vol. i, p. 581. See *infra*, chapter on special legislation.

[2] A similar provision was incorporated in the constitutions of South Dakota and Wyoming, adopted in 1889. The Kentucky constitution of 1892 declares, in section 156, that " The cities and towns of this Commonwealth, for the purposes of

The official report of the proceedings and debates of the convention does not indicate the party affiliations of the members. It is therefore impossible to tell whether the opinions in regard to the policy of municipal legislation divided along party lines as much as they did in the Michigan convention of 1867. However that may be, there was manifested a strong feeling in favor of local self-government in the debates. The members who favored general legislation put less emphasis on this phase of the problem, except in answer to the attacks of those who defended special legislation. The first great speech against the report of the committee was delivered by a gentleman from Cincinnati[1] while the convention was sitting at Columbus in the summer of 1873. His argument for special legislation was based on two grounds. First, the grant of a general borrowing power to cities and towns is dangerous, because it gives the local rings too much power. The localities ought to be compelled to come to the legislature whenever they want to borrow money, in order to preserve a legislative control over the municipal councils. Second, the way ought to be left open for the people of any locality to call on the legislature for protection against their local officers. It had

their organization and government, shall be divided into six classes. The organization and powers of each class shall be defined and provided for by general laws, so that all municipal corporations of the same class shall possess the same powers and be subject to the same restrictions." The limits of population for the six classes are then definitely fixed, and the general assembly is required to assign the cities and towns to their proper classes and change the assignment as population increases or decreases. These Kentucky provisions form the most elaborate attempt to prohibit special legislation for cities yet embodied in any state constitution. The New York constitution of 1894, while not prohibiting special legislation, defines the term " special act" in so many words, as any act applying to any lers than all the cities of a given class. The population limits of the several classes are fixed, the rank of each city to be determined by its population, according to the latest state enumeration, and all special acts are subjected to the suspensive veto power of the city authorities. They become law in spite of the local veto, if passed a second time by the legislature.

[1] Mr. John W. Herron, Debates of the Convention, vol. i, pp. 590–592.

been necessary, for instance, in the case of Cincinnati for the legislature to create a second chamber in the council to protect the city from the ring. Referring to the remarks of Mr. Hoadly already quoted, the gentleman went on to say: " Those laws, he said, every lawyer would regard as unconstitutional, and yet so completely were they in accordance with the wishes of the people, so necessary were they to the interests of those corporations, that but in one single instance was there found a citizen ready to go into the Supreme Court, and ask to have those laws declared unconstitutional. In one case, where it was undertaken to annex the village of Clifton to the city of Cincinnati, where the wealthy men of that suburb found that their taxes would be increased by annexation, they did employ my friend to apply to the Supreme Court, and *he* succeded in having that law declared unconstitutional, as being a case of special legislation.[1] . . . That is the only case within my recollection where the people have not been so thoroughly satisfied as to the correctness of the legislation, that a single one of them has ever attempted to have them set aside or declared illegal. Now, are we going to place a strait-jacket around every city and municipal corporation in this state? Are we going to say that every rule which we are applying to Cincinnati shall apply to Cleveland, if it has the same population, and that we shall fence them around by an iron barrier beyond which they shall not go? Shall we say that they are finished, that we can provide for all future time for all cities alike, and that they are all to be covered by one universal rule? I say you cannot do it; and I believe that system of tying up, this system of binding around every individual, every municipal corporation, has done more to retard the progress of Ohio than all the bad legislation that has ever been passed by the state. Why, sir, when you have children, you are willing to trust them sometimes to spend money; you are

---

[1] State *v.* Cincinnati, 20 Ohio St., 18.

willing that they should learn by experience whether they
have proper judgment in the spending of money or not. Why
will you not leave your municipal corporations, which are an
aggregate of individuals, to some judgment, to the exercise of
some discretion in the responsibility of spending money, as the
people of those corporations may prefer? Pass your general
laws regulating the manner in which they shall be governed,
but then leave your legislature with certain powers, either to
enlarge or diminish, to increase the facilities or to take them
away, as the circumstances of each case mny require."

In brief, the gentleman's proposition was this: The people
of the localities must be granted a large degree of self-government, but the right of central legislative control must be reserved in order to keep local financial undertakings within
proper limits and to protect the people of the localities from
the power of rings.

The second important argument against the attempt to prohibit special legislation for cities was delivered by another
delegate from Cincinnati,[1] and president of the convention,
when the subject was again taken up in February, 1874. In
the beginning of his speech he said: " The convention of
1851 attempted an impossibility. It sought to enforce uniformity upon the cities and villages of Ohio, by the passage of
this Thirteenth Article on corporations . . . What I object to
in the existing constitution, and in the proposition now before
us, is this idea of governing cities and villages upon the same
principle that you regulate banks, railroads, cotton factories
and private corporations of every sort ; thus assuming to place
the people of our cities or towns upon the same footing in respect to the great functions of municipal government, upon
which you administer the dollar-and-cent operations of private
corporations, created for mere trade and commerce."

After a warm eulogy upon the local self-government that

---

[1] Mr. Rufus King, Debates of the Convention, vol. ii, pt. 2, pp. 1299–1303.

obtained in Ohio cities prior to the constitution of 1851, the delegate said: " Of all this independence, which the people of Ohio were thus enjoying, the constitution of 1851 deprived us. It repealed at one stroke, and, so far as I can discover, without debate or murmur, the independent charters under which all our cities and towns were enjoying each their own little system of organization and management. Some gentleman, imbued with this central idea of French politics—who he was I do not know, for the record does not tell—put this thing in their bonnets, and it seems to have buzzed about like a bumble bee, till it got into the heads of everybody, and was passed without a dissenting voice. It undertook to amend every charter of every city and town in Ohio, and to compel the legislature to put them all under general and uniform laws.

"But, sir, it has proved a total failure. . . . The people of the state, the legislature, and the courts, have virtually re-pealed it long since, by evasions directly in violation of its letter and spirit. It could not be kept. . . . The only object which it was to subserve was to get rid of special legislation; but it has rather served to multiply such legislation, and has introduced confusion far worse than any that can be found under the legislation prior to 1851. Legislation has become so special and intricate, under these 'general laws,' that it is now almost impossible for any man, except he be a lawyer, and it is difficult even for many of them, to tell what the law is with regard to many points in municipal government. . . . I tried the other day to find a single and very simple point in the municipal law regulating the city of Cincinnati, and, after much effort, have not found it yet. It is said there was once a monarch, named Procrustes, who, by a general law, decreed every man in his kingdom to be of the same size, and he put them in a uniform machine which cut off their heads or their feet, just as circumstances required. It seems very much like the same thing when we require municipal governments in Ohio to be all of one and the same organization. It has proved a failure. The Legislature and the Supreme Court have disregarded it, and the people of Ohio are living in plain violation of their constitution. They have been compelled to violate their constitution. They cannot live under it; and the proposition now brought forward by the committee as a substitute is, in my judgment, calculated to make the evil worse than it already is. For, sir, while the Legislature and the courts have driven a coach and four through this uniformity clause in the present constitution, by a system of classification and circumlocution which has become the laughing-stock of the people of the state, it is now proposed to amend by dividing all the cities, towns and villages in Ohio into six classes, and to hedge in each of these classes by a cast-iron provision of the Procrustean sort, so terrible as to defy opposition."

A large part of this speech was devoted to the inevitable loss of local autonomy under a system of only general laws for cities in classes. The speaker laid especial emphasis on the trouble that each city would have to incur in defending its liberties before the Legislature whenever any city of the same class asked for a change in the general law. One paragraph is worth quoting: "The objection to the whole system is this, that it compels the different cities which must thus be grouped together into one class, to be perpetually interfering with each other, engaging in a constant, internecine war with each other, with regard to all of the small details of their home government. It necessarily puts them at war with each other upon every diversity which either or any of the class may seek from the Legislature in organization, power, or liabilities."

It is needless to follow the debate further in detail. The supporters of the proposition reported by the committee answered the objection that self-government and the demands of peculiar local conditions would be overthrown, by saying that general laws could be passed regulating the forms of city organization, while each particular city could be left free to exercise at will any privilege which the legislature should feel justified in granting to any city. It was evident to all that under general laws it would be impossible to provide for all the needs of all the localities on the basis of a detailed enumeration. But the majority of the convention desired to get rid of special legislation by all means, and so the section was passed as reported by the committee, leaving the problem of local autonomy under general laws to be solved by the Legislature.

Some other provisions of importance were adopted by the convention. Municipal corporations were forbidden to loan their credit, and the limit of indebtedness was fixed. Special assessments could not be made requiring a payment of more than ten per cent. of the taxable valuation of property in any one year, nor more than fifty per cent. of the highest taxable valuation in any period of ten years. These propositions also received their share of consideration and discussion. But although the debates of the convention furnished an important contribution to the study of municipal government,[1] they had no marked effect on the actual course of legislation, as the proposed constitution was not ratified at the polls.

The complete failure of the constitution of 1851 to do away with special legislation may have one of two effects. It may ultimately convince the people of Ohio that special laws for different cities are necessary, and any attempt to do away with them must end in failure. On the other hand the opponents of special legislation may be so much strengthened in their position that they will be willing, in practice as well as in theory, to modify the doctrine of enumerated powers, and make a new effort to compel the cities to accept a uniform municipal organization, while leaving them a large degree of freedom for meeting local emergencies in the exercise and direction of their administrative functions. It is not unlikely, however, if we are to judge from the opinions already held in the conven-

[1] See Ohio Convention Debates, 1873–1874, vol. i, pp. 578–595, vol. ii, pt. 2, pp. 1288–1441.

tion of 1873 and 1874, that each side will continue to become more convinced of the correctness of its own position for a good while to come.[1]   In what condition such a division of sentiment leaves the laws of the state, we shall see more fully in the following chapter.

[1] See Hon. E. J. Blandin's paper on *Uniform Organization for Cities in Ohio*, Proceedings of the Minneapolis and Cleveland Conferences for Good City Government, pp. 454–463.

CHAPTER V.

I. *The general laws of 1852 and 1853.*

By the constitution adopted in 1851 the General Assembly
of Ohio was forbidden to pass any special act conferring corporate powers,[1] and was required to provide for the organization of cities and incorporated villages by general laws.[2]   Ac-
cordingly, on May 3, 1852, a general municipal corporations
act was passed, the first of its kind in the United States.[3]   By
the first section of this act, all special charters then in force
were repealed, and all the municipal corporations of the State
were brought under the general law.

After establishing this method of forming new corporations,
this act enumerated in detail through twenty sections the
powers of all the municipalities excepting special road
districts.   The powers included the authority to establish
water works and cemeteries; to lay out, open and improve streets, public grounds, wharves and market places; to
construct sewers; to levy special assessments for street lighting and improvement; to make by-laws and ordinances, not inconsistent with state laws, to carry into effect the powers

---

[1] Art. xiii, sec. 1.   [2] *Ibid.*, sec. 6.

[3] Ohio Laws, 50 v. 223-259 (vol. l, pp. 223-259).   The Indiana Constitution
of 1851, art. xi, sec. 13, had forbidden special acts of incorporation.   But sec. 4 of
the schedule provided that special municipal charters should continue in force
until modified or repealed by the general assembly.   The Indiana law of June
18, 1852 (Ind. Laws, 1852, vol. ii, pp. 203-221), was not made to apply, therefore, to cities already incorporated, unless they chose to come under its provisions.

granted; and a long list of police powers. A general clause granted the authority to pass such ordinances " as to them shall seem necessary to provide for the safety, preserve the health, promote the prosperity, and improve the morals, order, comfort and convenience of such corporations and the inhabitants thereof."

In the next division the classification of municipal corporations was provided. Cities of more than 20,000 population were to constitute the first class, and cities from 5,000 to 20,000, the second class. Other municipal corporations were classed as incorporated villages, and incorporated villages for special purposes, or special road districts. In the year following each Federal census, it was made the duty of the Governor, Auditor and Secretary of State to ascertain those cities and villages entitled by increase of population to be advanced to the next higher class. After the list had been published, the councils of the municipalities affected were required to take the necessary steps for reorganization in the new class.

The corporate power of villages was vested in a mayor, a recorder and five trustees, who together formed the village council, and were given the power of further organization of village offices. In cities, there were to be a mayor, and a city council composed of two trustees elected from each ward. Other officers were named, the list being somewhat different for the two classes of cities. The city council was required to appoint, or provide for the election of all officers, whether mentioned in the act or afterwards established by ordinance. All cities might establish a police force, fire companies and a board of health. In cities of the first class the " board system " was introduced. There were to be elected three water-works trustees, three city commissioners, and three infirmary directors. There might also be established a board of directors for the house of refuge. Together with the mayor and civil engineer, the city commissioners were to form a board of city improvements, under the direction of the council.

Detailed limitations were placed on the taxing and the borrowing powers. No loans could be made except in anticipation of yearly revenues. These loans could not exceed the following amounts:—for special road districts, $1,000; for villages, $5,000; for cities of the second class, $50,000; for cities of the first class, $100,000. In the same way, the tax limits for general and incidental expenses were fixed for the four grades of municipalities at two and a half, three, three and five mills on the dollar of valuation respectively.[1] The collection of taxes was to be made by the county treasurer, after the rate had been fixed by the municipal authorities and reported to the county auditor.

Such was Ohio's first general law for cities and villages. In the next year, 1853, a supplementary and amendatory act was passed,[2] containing about a third as many sections as the law of the previous year. One provision of importance was that which gave city councils full power to fix and alter the ward boundaries. Aside from this the two chief points of this act were connected with the advancement from class to class, and the financial powers of municipal corporations. It was provided that the consent of the council should be required before any city or village was advanced to the next higher grade, and upon petition of the council with evidence of the required population a city could be advanced between decennial periods. A tax of four mills on the dollar was allowed in cities of the

---

[1] For cities, special tax levies were permitted as follows: Cities of the second class, police fund and fire department fund, each one mill; cities of the first class, police fund, two mills; fire department fund, one mill; house of refuge, house of correction, workhouse, and city prison, one and a half mills; water works, one-half mill; schools, two mills; city infirmary and poor relief, two mills. An extra one-half mill tax was allowed to all municipal corporations for a sinking fund. Also all municipal councils were required to levy an interest fund tax, not exceeding two mills on the dollar, to pay interest on all outstanding debts. It was further permitted to levy a tax on dogs and other animals not on the state and county tax list.

[2] O. L., 51 v., 360–374.

second class for school purposes. For paying off existing indebtedness, villages could levy a seven-mill tax, while the
limit of the required interest fund tax was raised from two to
six mills. Municipal corporations were given the right to
refund their debts, where they could not be paid under the
tax limitations. Cities of the first class, not already having
water works, were authorized to borrow $500,000 for that
purpose, with the approval of the electors, the details of the
loan to be determined by the council. The council of any city
of the first class was also permitted to borrow $500,000 for
the purchase of lands for public wharves, squares, parks or
market places, on conditions fixed in the law with a good deal
of stringency. The borrowing power was granted to the
councils of all municipal corporations for the purchase of
school grounds and the erection of school buildings.

These two acts of 1852 and 1853 formed the general foundation for the system of municipal legislation that was to grow
up under the constitutional prohibition of special legislation.
It is significant that by the first law the idea of classification
by population was introduced, while by the second, advancement from one class to another with increase of population
was made optional with each locality. From this resulted the
present confusion of Ohio classification. By the census of
1850, only Cincinnati had more than 20,000 population, but by
1853, Cleveland was ready to be assigned to the first class of
cities. Since then only one city, Toledo, has availed itself of
the privilege of promotion from the second to the first class,
although by the census of 1890 there were ten cities in Ohio
with more than 20,000 population each. While on this side
we see the reason for Ohio's intricate classification, if we consider the taxing and borrowing regulations of these first general laws, it becomes plain that new legislation would be
needed if the cities were to develop freely. The limitations of
the tax levies, and the general denial of the borrowing power,
led inevitably to a great mass of special legislation in the years
following.

In regard to the provision of the law granting the right of redistricting each city to that city's council, we may quote from the convention debates of 1873, where a delegate illustrated the demand for special legislation from the history of his own city. He said: " We had in Cincinnati what was a complete rotten borough system. One ward had a voting population of 200 ; another had a voting population of 2,500. Less than one-third of the city controlled the entire election; less than one-third of the population elected a majority of the members of the Council and Board of Aldermen. Your general law provided how the districting of the city should be done. It was left to the city council, the very body elected under this system, and year after year an appeal was made to redistrict the city into wards of nearly equal population. It was found impossible to obtain it from them ; and this rotten borough system continued year after year, until, as a last resort, the people appealed to the legislature for relief, and what the gentleman calls a special act was passed, directing the redistricting of the city in a special way."[1]

II. *Growth of special legislation prior to the municipal code of 1869.*

The first step towards introducing special acts into the forms of the general law took the form of acts referring to all cities with more or less than a given population, thus bringing a special population classification within the general classification of the original statutes. The first example of this kind was the law of April 5, 1856, which applied to cities of the first class having less than 80,000 population by the last federal census, or any succeeding census.[2] This was an important measure, changing the organization of Cleveland in quite a radical manner. Another act of the same year made a special tax limit for cities of more than 100,000 inhabitants by the last

[1] Convention Debates of 1873–74, vol. i, p. 591.

[2] O. L., 53 v. 57–59.

federal census.[1] A law of 1859 conferred powers upon the
Cleveland council, being addressed to every city of the first
class *then having* less than 80,000 and more than 35,000 population.[2] Soon afterwards, by an avowedly local and special
act, the Cleveland board of education was organized, and
given various powers and duties which were partly dependent
on the city council for approval, direction or completion.[3] The
Supreme Court decided later that boards of education and
school districts were not corporate bodies within the meaning
of the constitution.[4] But those parts of this law conferring
powers of oversight upon the city council were certainly in violation of the constitution. An act of 1861 introduced important changes into the city government of Cleveland, applying
only to such cities of the first class having less than 80,000 inhabitants as should be of that class when the law went into
effect, which was to be immediately after its passage.[5] It is
important to notice that this law, though general in form, was
so drawn that it could never apply to more than one city,
Cleveland. Two years later cities of the second class which
had more than 13,000 population at the last census were specially empowered to construct sewers.[6] Three cities, Columbus,
Dayton, and Toledo, fell within this category.

The tide of special legislation had now set in with much
force. I have given only a few examples to show the various
forms it was beginning to assume. In 1863, eleven acts were
passed referring to municipal corporations, eight of which applied to less than all of one class. Ohio's future descriptive
ingenuity was but dimly foreshadowed in an act fixing the
tax limit in cities of the second class with a population of
not less than 13,000 at the last federal census, and having an
amount of taxable property on the grand duplicate not exceed-

---

[1] O. L., 53 v. 214.   [2] *Ibid.*, 56 v. 127.
[3] *Ibid.*, 56 v. 281.   [4] State *v.* Powers, 38 Ohio St., 54.
[5] O. L., 58 v. 25.   [6] *Ibid.*, 60 v. 6.

ing six million dollars.[1] During the years following 1860, a good many special acts were passed, conferring various kinds of powers on sundry cities and villages; as for instance, authorizing the city of Hamilton to borrow money,[2] the council of Greenfield to appropriate certain moneys,[3] the city council of Zanesville to construct a market house,[4] the city council of Mansfield to sell or lease certain lands,[5] the city of Tiffin to levy a tax,[6] to change the boundaries of Zanesville,[7] to legalize the municipal corporation known as the town of Massillon.[8] This kind of legislation became much more common in later years, until it was partially checked by the decisions of the Supreme Court.

In 1864, for purposes of tax limitation, villages were divided into those with more and those with less than 2,500 population.[9] The confusing effect of the option clause of the act of 1853 with reference to advancement began to be apparent when laws were enacted for cities of the second class, having less than 20,000 population.[10] There would have been no second class cities with a greater population than 20,000, except for the fact that any city, once in a class, might choose to stay there always. Dayton, by the census of 1860, was entitled to become a city of the first class, but had not chosen to be advanced. From time to time, the population limit in laws intended for Cincinnati was increased so as to shut out Cleveland. Before 1870, the usual form came to be, all cities of the first class having upwards of 150,000 population.[11] It was becoming evident that differences in population were only the excuse for a classification really based on differences in geographical location and industrial development. One of the distinctly special acts of this period, clothed in general form,

---

[1] O. L., 60 v. 95.   [2] *Ibid.*, 57 v. 141.   [3] *Ibid.*, 60 v. 124.

[4] *Ibid.*, 60 v. 121.   [5] *Ibid.*, 59 v. 130.   [6] *Ibid.*, 63 v. 222.

[7] *Ibid.*, 59 v. 123.   [8] *Ibid.*, 61 v. 146.   [9] *Ibid.*, 61 v. 100.

[10] *Ibid.*, 61 v. 72, 62 v. 135.   [11] *Ibid.*, 63 v. 189–190, 64 v. 7–8.

but affecting Toledo alone, referred to all cities advanced in grade to the first class between decennial periods, and prior to May, 1867.[1] Dayton was singled out by two acts, one referring to all cities of the *second* class having over 20,000 population,[2] and the other referring to " any city having a population of less than 25,000, and more than 20,000 at the last federal census."[3] "Any city of the second class, situated in any county having a population of more than 42,000 inhabitants at the last federal census, the commissioners whereof shall have been empowered to erect a court house," was authorized to levy a tax and give $25,000 towards this enterprise.[4] There were four counties with the population named, each containing a city of the second class. It only remained for the legislature to authorize one of them to build a court house, and the law just referred to would become very special at once. Another act permitted " the council of any incorporated village having taxable property exceeding $100,000 and less than $125,000," to establish a cemetery on certain conditions.[5] A law of April 13, 1868,[6] said in section one : " The city council of any city of the first class, having a population exceeding 150,000, shall have the power to issue the bonds of such city, in any sum not exceeding $150,000, to be used for the purpose of completing the Eggleston avenue sewer." Section three said : " Whenever any of the bonds herein provided for shall be for sale, not less than ten days' previous notice of said sale shall be advertised in Cincinnati." During the five years from 1864 to 1868 inclusive, eighty acts, general in form, were passed, making special classifications of cities and villages ; while fifty-six other acts recognized the general classification adopted in the law of 1852.

It would seem by this time that an observer must begin to

---

[1] O. L., 64 v. 52.   See also 65 v. 104–106.   [2] *Ibid.*, 64 v. 121.

[3] *Ibid.*, 64 v. 123.   [4] *Ibid.*, 64 v. 129.

[5] *Ibid.*, 64 v. 203.   [6] *Ibid.*, 65 v. 86.

doubt the existence of a court of law in Ohio, to which the interpretation of the constitution could be referred. But in the December term of 1868, the Supreme Court decided the case of Welker *vs.* Potter.[1] A law passed in 1866, conferring certain powers in regard to street improvements upon cities of the first class with less than 100,000 population at the last federal census,[2] was *upheld* by this decision. The constitutional provision considered was the one requiring that "all laws of a general nature shall have a uniform operation throughout the state."[3] Nine years later, in the case of The State *vs.* Mitchell,[4] the court explained that in this earlier case the question of granting corporate powers by special act had not been brought up or considered at all. This decision made in 1868, after twelve years of really special legislation, was not calculated to instil in the minds of Ohio law-makers any new respect for the constitutional limitations requiring general legislation. The laws of 1869 speak for themselves. By one, "the city council of any city of the second class having a population exceeding 20,000 and not exceeding 20,100, at the last federal census," was authorized to issue bonds for the payment of its debt.[5] The act of May 6th is quite a curiosity.[6] Here is the first section: "The city council of any city of the first class having a population of 150,000 inhabitants, wherein a public avenue of not less than one hundred feet in width is now projected, to be known as 'Gilbert avenue,' is hereby authorized to issue the bonds of said city in any sums not exceeding $150,-000, for improving such avenue, bearing a rate of interest not to exceed seven and three-tenths per cent. per annum at such dates and for such length of time as they may deem expedient, the same to be sold at not less than par, and the proceeds thereof to be applied exclusively to the improvement of such

[1] 18 Ohio St., 85.　　　　　　　[2] O. L., 63 v. 133.

[3] Cons., art. ii, sec. 26.　　　　　[4] 31 Ohio St., 592.

[5] O. L., 66 v. 144.　　　　　　　[6] *Ibid.*, 66 v. 130.

' Gilbert avenue' commencing at the western terminus of said
avenue."

On the very next day after this last act was passed, the
general municipal code of 1869, containing sixty-one chapters
and 732 sections, became a law.[1]   At the end, a list of 185
acts were enumerated and repealed. The object seems to
have been the codification and unification of the really general
laws, with no pretense of putting an end to special legislation.
This conclusion finds weighty support in the wording of an
act passed at the opening of the legislative session of 1870,
which authorized the council, " in cities of the second class,
containing a population of 9,229, and no more, according to
the census of 1860," to build a railway within the corporate
limits.[2]

III. *Special legislation since 1870 under the influence of Supreme Court decisions.*

In the December term of 1870, a case[3] was brought to the
Supreme Court involving the constitutionality of a special act
passed in the preceding April, " to prescribe the corporate
limits of the city of Cincinnati."[4]   As a matter of fact, by this
law the boundaries of the city had been extended to cover
considerable outlying territory in which were included several
incorporated villages. The act was declared void, and the
court put forward these three propositions : (1) The General
Assembly cannot, by special act, create a corporation. (2) It
cannot, by special act, confer corporate powers on corporations already existing. (3) In the purview of these propositions and of the constitutional provisions on which they are
based, there is no distinction between private and municipal
corporations. In the following session of the general assembly, 1871, it seems that two-thirds of the laws, general in

---

[1] O. L., 66 v. 145–286.   [2] *Ibid.*, 67 v. 11.
[3] The State *v.* The City of Cincinnati, 20 Ohio St., 18.
[4] O. L., 67 v. 141.

form, referring to municipalities, respected the established classification. Several laws affected cities with over 150,000 or 180,000 population. One referred to those with from 11,000 to 12,000 population.[1] For purposes of tax limitation villages were classed as those with more and those with less than 3,000 population.[2] In each of the two classes of cities there were made three grades, the population limits of the first class, third grade, being exactly the same as of the second class, first grade—30,000 to 80,000.

The practice of the Supreme Court in deciding that certain acts brought before it were not unconstitutional under other provisions, without considering the question involved in conferring corporate powers affecting only one city, doubtless led to a good deal of confusion for several years as to the real attitude of the court toward classification. The case of Walker *vs.* Cincinnati[3], decided in 1871, like that of Welker *vs.* Potter[4], already referred to, was such a case. The act conferring upon cities of the first class with 150,000 inhabitants the right to construct a railroad, under which the " Cincinnati Southern" was established, was held not to be in conflict with those sections of the constitution cited in the argument. Of course, it is impossible to determine just how much the legislature was influenced by these decisions. But whatever the cause, its disregard for the constitution was always a progressive factor in its municipal law-making. In three acts of the year 1872, Cleveland, which had a population of 92,000, was the only city included within the different limits, 50,000 to 100,000, 80,000 to 100,000 and 90,000 to 150,000.[5] But the climax of that year's legal fictions was reached when " villages or cities containing a population of 5,641, and no more, by the federal census of 1870, published in the last volume of the Ohio Statistical Report," were authorized to erect car shops.[6]

[1] O. L., 68 v. 132.   [2] *Ibid.*, 68 v. 133.

[3] 21 Ohio St., 14.   [4] 18 Ohio St., 85, *supra*.

[5] O. L., 69 v. 13, 128, 138.   [6] *Ibid.*, 69 v. 70.

It is only very slowly that judicial light penetrated into this legal jungle. An important step was taken, however, in the second case of the State *vs.* The City of Cincinnati.[1] Several years before, a special act had been passed establishing the Cincinnati Commercial Hospital, and putting it under the management of a board of trustees, with power to issue by-laws and regulations for its government.[2] By a subsequent act these rules and regulations were subjected to the approval of the city council before going into effect.[3] The Court upheld the former act,[4] as not establishing a corporation, but declared the later act unconstitutional as conferring corporate powers on the city council by special act. These decisions, however, not yet touching the question of classification, had no deterrent effect on the Assembly. Toledo, with a population of 31,584, was differentiated from Columbus, whose inhabitants numbered 31,274, not only by being in a different class, but also by the population line fixed at 31,500[5]. Xenia was any city of the second class having a population at the last federal census not exceeding 6,400, nor less than 6,300.[6] A law was passed to affect all cities and villages through which the National Road passed.[7] In 1876, a law was passed regulating the general tax for street improvements, to appply to all cities except cities of the first class, " having at the last federal census of A. D. 1870, a population of not less than 31,500, nor more than 33,000."[8]

In the years 1874 to 1876 there were passed at least nineteen acts which, though general in phraseology, never could apply to more than one city. One of these provided that " in all cities of the first class, having at the last federal census a population of 200,000 and over, the police powers and duties

---

[1] 23 Ohio St., 445.   [2] O. L., 58 v. 151.   [3] *Ibid.*, 61 v. 142.

[4] The State of Ohio *v.* Davis, 23 Ohio St., 434, argued in connection with the other case.

[5] O. L., 70 v. 117, 142.   [6] *Ibid.*, 70 v. 116.

[7] *Ibid.*, 70 v. 153.   [8] *Ibid.*, 72 v. 24.

shall be invested in and exercised by a board of five members
to be appointed by the governor."[1]   This act was tested before the Supreme Court in the case of The State *vs.* Covington;[2]
and held to be valid on the ground that this police board was
not made a corporate body, and hence was not given corporate powers.   Referring to the phraseology of the act as
probably intended to protect it from the constitutional provision, the court said :   " If such was the purpose, it is well to
say here that such ends cannot be accomplished by such means.
This enactment is essentially local and special in its nature.
We do not deny that the legislature may classify the subjects
of legislation—to wit, cities and villages—and that a statute in
relation to a class would be treated as a general law, within
the meaning of these provisions of the constitution, but there
is no classification accomplished by this statute.   Cincinnati
was, is, and ever will be, the only city in this state that had a
population of 200,000 and over at the federal census of 1870.
Cincinnati therefore is the only city to which this statute can
ever apply, and it might as well have been named in the act."
But the court held that local legislation is not prohibited by
the constitution unless it be of a general nature, or be special
legislation conferring corporate power.   Hence, although the
circumlocution of the general assembly was rebuked, the way
was laid open for the transfer of all the public functions of
cities and villages to boards or individiduals not responsible to
the corporation in any way, and this could be done boldly
without any pretense of general forms.[3]   A year later, in the
case of The State *vs.* Mitchell,[4] the court carried its dictum

---

[1] O. L., 73 v. 70.   [2] 29 Ohio St., 102.

[3] See also, The State *v.* Davis, 23 Ohio St., 434, *supra.*

[4] 31 Ohio St., 592, *supra.*   This case is a good one, as showing how far the
courts will go to protect the innocent holders of bonds issued under an unconstitutional statute.   The law had provided that the abutting owners on any street
might petition for the benefits of the act, and elect commissioners to superintend
certain improvements desired to be made. The city was to issue bonds in advance
to pay for the work, and special assessments were to be levied to pay the bonds.
The court held that where the bonds had been issued and the improvements com-

into effect by holding an act invalid which had attempted to confer upon the council of Columbus certain powers in regard to street improvements, under the guise of cities of the second class having above 31,000 population at the last census. The fatal clause in the act was, " at the last federal census." The attitude of the court certainly bewildered the General Assembly. For whereas in 1877, before the last decision, laws had been passed applying to any cities of the second class in this state which by the last federal census had " a population of 12,652" [1] and " a population of not more than 11,082 nor less than 11,080,"[2] in the year following an extra appropriation from the school fund for the support of public libraries was authorized " in all cities which, by the last federal census, had, and all those which hereafter, on the first day of March, in any year, as ascertained by any federal census, may have a population exceeding 90,000 and less than 200,000 inhabitants."[3] This certainly was a general law according to the rules of the court, but it conferred powers on the board of education which by a later decision turned out to be no corporate body at all within the meaning of the constitution. This is an excellent illustration of the spasmodic attempts on the part of the law-makers to bring now and then an act within the provisions of the constitution in the spirit of the court's interpretation. But when at the same session, mixed in with a few such attempts, we find many of the old palpable violations repeated, and other violations of the spirit of the law as glaring as an act which actually authorized " any incorporated village, which, by the federal census of 1870, had, and which, by any subsequent federal census, may have a population of 1087 "[4] to borrow money for railway construction, it seems utterly inconceivable that all these acts were voted on and passed by the same assembly.

pleted, all the owners who had in any way participated in the proceedings leading to the execution of the work, were estopped from pleading the unconstitutionality of the act in order to avoid paying their assessments.

[1] O. L., 74 v. 174.   [2] *Ibid.*, 74 v. 203.   [3] *Ibid.*, 75 v. 11.   [4] *Ibid.*, 75 v. 110.

On May 14, 1878, a new municipal code was enacted.[1]   In
it we find the intricate system of classification which still remains as the groundwork of Ohio legislation.   Cities of the
first class were divided into three grades, with provision for a
fourth grade to be composed of cities afterwards advanced
from the second class.   Cities of the second class were divided into four grades.   Villages were divided into two
classes.   As in the laws of 1852 and 1853, villages could be
advanced to cities of the second class when their population
exceeded 5,000, and second-class cities could become first-
class cities when their population exceeded 20,000.   But advancement was optional, and there certainly were no very
great inducements held out for the exercise of the option, in
the shape of liberal legislation.   It seems, further, that the advancement from grade to grade within the class was not
optional.   The wording of the section has a peculiar Ohio
twang.   Grades were to be determined by the formula—
" Those which, on the first day of July last, had, and those
which hereafter, on the first day of July in any year, have, according to any official report or abstract of the then next preceding federal census," a population of over 200,000 shall constitute the first grade, between 90,000 and 200,000 the second
grade, and between 31,500 and 90,000 the third grade of the
first class ; between 30,500 and 31,500 the first grade, between
20,000 and 30,500 the second grade, between 10,000 and
20,000 the third grade, and below 10,000 the fourth grade of
the second class.   The first five grades included one city each,
and it was very evident that the population basis was simply
incidental.   It seems that the only way in which a particular
grade could be recruited was by cities coming up from a lower
class.   For the cities which had a population within the respective limits at the time of the act, that is, by the census of
1870, were to remain in their grades as then assigned.   At
least, so it worked in practice as recognized by later laws, and

[1] O. L., 75 v. 161–419.

no provision was made for voluntary advancement from grade
to grade.   The code embodied in its later divisions, with little
change, the already existing laws passed from time to time.
At the end, 123 acts were enumerated and repealed.   On the
same day acts were passed for cities with 10,592[1] and 8,075[2]
population respectively at the last census.

After a quarter of a century of experiment and struggle
against an oppressive constitution and a capricious Supreme
Court, at last the assembly had succeeded in laying down the
main lines of municipal law-making.   With the five chief
cities each settled in its own grade for all time with moral
certainty, it only remained necessary to add a new grade from
time to time as some smaller town rose to prominence, and in
the case of villages and less important cities, to describe them
by their population at the last census with the redeeming clause
which made the law applicable to corporatins with the same
population at any future census.   It was even deemed safe to
grant a margin of two, five or ten inhabitants, and in some
cases still more.   It was an exciting play with chance.   I
imagine that many an hour has passed swiftly for Ohio legislators as they busied themselves with the pleasing mathemat-
ical problem of how much latitude in population could be given
in any particular act without incurring the calamitous prob-
ability that more than one city or village would come within
its scope in the course of a century.   The Ohio legislature
had won a splendid triumph.   The situation was so completely
in its own hands that there was no need to adopt the form of
general legislation in most cases referring to villages and
minor cities.   Duriug the seventeen years from 1876 to 1892
inclusive, more than 1200 special acts were passed granting
by name to strictly municipal corporations the right to issue
bonds for every imaginable purpose, to transfer certain specified funds, to build halls, to sell or buy land, to build bridges,
to construct sewers, to levy special taxes, to improve streets,

[1] O. L., 75 v. 541.   [2] *Ibid.*, 75 v. 557.

to erect gas works, to extend water works, to establish a police force, to procure fire engines, to sink natural gas wells, etc., etc., including a few acts changing the corporate name. These acts could be passed with impunity, either because the citizens of the localities were indifferent, or because by the simple application of the cure-all formula any one of the acts could be made general, if any symptoms of opposition appeared. In practice there was much variation from year to year in the number of these acts. From fifty-four in 1877 they fell to twenty-four in 1880, climbed to fifty-four again in 1883, and reached their maximum at one hundred and seventy-six in 1889, dropping to eighty-one in 1892, and rising again to eighty-eight in 1894. Of the 1202 such acts passed between 1876 and 1892, 594 gave power to borrow money, 470 gave power to transfer funds, and 60 gave power to levy a special tax, making a total of 1124 or 93.5 per cent. giving special financial powers to the cities and villages named in the acts.[1]   No better proof is needed that the most difficult

[1] *Local and Special Acts of the Ohio Legislature Conferring Powers upon Municipal Corporations.*

Year.	Total number of acts.	Conferring financial powers.	To borrow money.	To transfer funds.	To levy tax.
1876	11	7	3	1	3
1877 . . .	54	49	25	15	9
1878	41	35	22	9	4
1879	43	37	17	15	5
1880	24	20	6	10	4
1881	31	24	15	8	1
1882	24	24	9	4	11
1883	54	53	38	15	0
1884 . . .	56	52	26	24	2
1885	62	59	38	18	3
1886	66	61	31	27	3
1887	80	75	46	26	3
1888	117	109	51	56	2
1889	176	168	1c5	58	5
1890	126	121	56	62	3
1891	156	151	72	77	2
1892	81	79	34	45	0
1876–92. . .	1202	1124	594	470	60

problem to solve by general municipal laws is the proper limitation upon the local financial powers, in a system where there
is no state control over the localities except that exercised by
the legislature.

It seems hardly necessary to follow through, from 1878 on,
the acts special in effect, but general in form. However, there
were added from year to year some new variations in the form-
ulæ of circumlocution, which we may consider for a moment.
In 1881 certain powers were conferred upon " the council of
any city of this state which by the federal census of 1880 had
a population entitling it to pass from the rank of a city of the
third grade, second class, into the rank of a city of the second
grade, second class, but which has provided by ordinance that
such city shall remain a city of the third grade, second class."[1]
The way in which a law is made to apply to various cities is
well illustrated by the act of April 16, 1883, establishing a
board of tax commissioners " in each city of the first, second
and third grades of the first class, and in cities of the second
class, first grade, and in cities having a population of 20,000,
and not more than 30,000, and in cities having a population of
15,435, by the last federal census." [2]   Two years later an act
authorized the issue of bonds by "the city councils of cities of
the second class, in which a majority of the electors, within
three years last past, have voted in favor of the erection of a
market house in *said city*, and which, from any cause, has not
been erected therein."[3]   Sometimes the name of the city affected was given in the title of the act, though in the act itself
it was referred to by its grade and class.   It was enacted in
1885, that " any city of the second grade of the first class is
hereby authorized to issue bonds to an amount not exceeding
$65,000, to provide means to construct and rebuild a bridge
over Walworth Run, on Pearl street, in the city of Cleveland."[4]

[1] O. L., 78 v. 178.   [2] *Ibid.*, 80 v. 124.
[3] *Ibid.*, 82 v. 90.   [4] *Ibid.*, 82 v. 114.

About two weeks later, a law affecting Dayton, provided, " That the city *councils of cities* of the second grade of the second class be and *is* hereby authorized and empowered, for the purposes herein set forth to issue bonds upon the terms herein named, entitled as follows, and to the amount severally set forth: Park street sewer bonds, $65,000; Southwestern sewerage bonds, $35,000. Said Park street bonds to be issued to enable the city council of said city to construct a sewer or drain, beginning at the Miami river and running through Apple, Oak and Ford streets, and through and along the present course of what is known as the Park street sewer, Parrott street drain and Steel's drains, to take the surface drainage water off of the southern and eastern parts of said city ; said southwestern sewerage bonds being issued to enable the city council of said city to construct drains for the purpose of draining the surface water from Power street, South Broadway and Euclid avenues, and the southern and western parts of said city." [1] Bad grammar is certainly not the worst feature of such legislation, though it does point to ignorance or carelessness not complimentary to the general assembly of one of the most populous states in the Union.

In 1886 a special tax levy was authorized " in any city of the fourth grade of the second class having by the last federal census a population of not less than 12,258, and not more than 13,000, and in which city there is established and maintained by a public library association, not organized for profit, a public library free to all the inhabitants of such city, and containing not less than 2,000 volumes."[2] This description goes into enough detail to identify an escaped convict. Another instance of such description is found in an act authorizing the issue of bonds to purchase a site and erect normal school buildings by " the council of any incorporated village in this state, wherein, at the time of the passage of this act, there exists a private corporation, not for profit, incorporated under

[1] O. L., 82 v. 129.   [2] *Ibid.,* 83 v. 79.

the general incorporation laws of this state, and the purpose
for which said incorporation is formed is to secure to its members and patrons the advantages of education in all departments of learning and knowledge, especially in the branches
usually comprehended in academic and university collegiate
courses, though not excluding such primary instruction as is
usually furnished in common and normal schools."[1]   A good
many acts were passed at various times affecting villages in
counties containing cities of a certain class and grade.   One
applied to all villages in Wood county,[2] authorizing them to
sink gas wells.   A law of April 12, 1889, was to the effect,
that " in cities of the third grade of the second class, which
were advanced to said third grade, second class, during the
year of our Lord 1887, and which had, according to a census
taken in such cities in compliance with the provisions of
chapter four, division two, Title XII, Revised Statutes, a population of 10,221 on the twentieth day of May in the said
year of our Lord, 1887, there shall be a board of public
affairs."[3]

The position of defiance toward court and constitution taken
so constantly and so successfully by the assembly needs no
better proof than the act of March 24, 1890, which provided,
" that in any village, situated in a county containing a city of
the first grade of the first class, which has been heretofore
specifically empowered by a special act of the legislature to
issue bonds for the purpose of purchasing a suitable site and
erecting thereon a building containing a town hall and offices
for the officers of the corporation, and said act has been found
to be unconstitutional because of conferring corporate powers
by special act, that the village council of any such village is
hereby authorized to issue the bonds of the said village, not
exceeding in amount $17,000, to sell the same and use the
proceeds thereof in purchasing a suitable site, and erecting

---

[1] O. L., 84 v. 63.   [2] *Ibid.*, 86 v. 429.   [3] *Ibid.*, 86 v. 246.

thereon a building containing a town hall and offices for the officers of the corporation."[1]   And yet at this same session of the assembly eight village councils were authorized by name to erect town halls.

The classification of cities had by no means reached its maximum of incomprehensibility in the municipal code of 1878. Although that law had evidently contemplated the possibility of cities being advanced from the second class to the first, in providing that such cities should constitute the fourth grade of the first class, no laws were ever provided for this empty grade. In 1888, however, the general assembly enacted that whenever a city of the second class should by vote of the people become a city of the fourth grade of the first class, it should be governed by its own laws then in force until new laws were enacted for its new grade.[2]   There is no evidence that such laws were enacted, and I see no particular inducement under the circumstances for any second class city willing its own promotion, unless perhaps there is prestige to be gained by the mere fact of being a city of the first class in Ohio.   But in 1891 the legislature put Springfield into a grade by itself, the third grade *a* of the second class, comprising all cities with a population between 28,000 and 33,000 at the census of 1890, or at future censuses.[3]   In 1894, cities between 16,000 and 18,000 were constituted the third grade *b* of the second class.[4]   Hamilton was the town affected.   Ashtabula, being all the cities with a population between 8,330 and 9,050, was made the fourth grade *a* of the same class.[5]   Although there appears to be some confusion in section 1548 of the statutes as last revised, the actual status of the chief cities as recognized by the legislature, with their population by the census of 1890, seems to be as presented in the accompanying

[1] O. L., 87 v. 94.　　　[2] *Ibid.*, 85 v. 130.　　　[3] *Ibid.*, 88 v. 159.

[4] *Ibid.*, 91 v. 14.　　　　　　[5] *Ibid.*, 91 v. 58.

table.[1] The last column shows the number of acts referring to these cities specially, passed at the legislative session of 1894. The total number of such acts passed would be something less than 176, the sum of the figures in the column, because in several cases two or three cities were specified by their particular grades or populations in the same act. These figures, of course, do not include the special acts for villages designated by population. Of these there were in 1891 as many as thirty-five. One of the confusing results of this way of naming villages and cities by population, is that the same method has been applied to counties and townships, although they are not held to be corporations in the meaning of the constitutional

[1] *Table Showing the Classification of Ohio Cities, 1894.*

	Grade.	Population basis of classificaton.	By which census.	Names of cities.	Population in 1890.	Number of acts referring to, passed in 1894.
First Class	1	200,000+	1870	Cincinnati.	296,908	43
	2	90,000– 200,000	1870	Cleveland.	261,353	22
	3	31,500–90,000	1870	Toledo.	81,434	14
	4	20,000–31,500[1]	Any	None.		
Second Class	1	30,500–31,500	1870	Columbus.	88,150	10
	2	20,000–30,500	1870	Dayton.	61,220	12
	3	10,000–20,000	1870	Youngstown.	33,220	4
				Akron.	27,601	2
				Canton.	26,189	2
				Zanesville.	21,009	5
				Sandusky.	18,471	0
				Newark.	14,270	1
				Portsmouth.	12,394	1
				Perhaps 9 others.	10.092 to 18,553	10
	3a	28,000–33,000	1890	Springfield.	31,897	6
	3b	16,000–18,000	1890	Hamilton.	17,565	8
	4	5,000–10,000	1870	Bellaire.	9,934	0
				Piqua.	9,090	1
				Marion.	8,327	2
				Marietta.	8,273	6
				Perhaps 24 others.	5247 to 8224	24
	4a	8,330–9,050	1890	Ashtabula.	8,338	3

[1] This is an inference fro.n the other provisions of the law.

restriction. Another peculiar phenomenon is the passage of precisely similar laws sometimes under this general population formula, and sometimes under the undisguised names of the municipalities as avowedly special acts. This certainly must be the result of the local origin of local acts, those drafting the measures in many cases being ignorant of the attitude and decisions of the Supreme Court on the subject of special legislation conferring corporate powers.

IV. *The doctrines of the Supreme Court.*

Even a general study of special legislation in Ohio under the constitution of 1850 would not be complete without going a little more fully into the decisions of the Supreme Court than I have done in the preceding pages. Perhaps the following summary of the rules already established will serve as a convenient presentation of the main points in the decisions of the court, if supplemented by a little explanation of the principal cases not referred to already.

(1) Local legislation is not prohibited by the constitution.[1]

(2) The constitutional prohibition of special acts conferring corporate power, applies to private and municipal corporations without distinction.[2]

(3) School districts and boards of education partake of the public nature of the county and the township, and are not corporate bodies in the meaning of the constitution.[3]

---

[1] State *v.* Covington, 29 Ohio St., 102, *supra.*

[2] State *v.* Cincinnati, 20 Ohio St., 18, *supra.*

[3] State *v.* Powers, 38 Ohio St., 54. In this case the general assembly had created a special school district, and provided for the election of a board of education, to whom property was to be transferred, and who were to have power to levy taxes, and all other powers belonging to " village districts," which were declared to be corporate bodies in the general law. The court said, " It is quite obvious to us that county and township organizations, altnough *quasi* corporations, are not within the meaning of this provision of the constitution ; and, upon full consideration, we are unanimous in the opinion that school districts, as similar organizations, though declared by statute to be bodies politic and corporate, are not within the

(4) Whether or not certain powers granted by the general assembly are corporate powers, depends largely upon the nature of the body upon which they are conferred.[1]

(5) It is competent for the assembly to establish special boards for specified cities, to be appointed by the governor or otherwise, independent of the municipal corporation, to which public governmental functions, such as the police, are given without incorporation.[2]

(6) The fact that certain officers were everywhere chosen by the people of the localities at the time that the constitution was adopted, does not operate as a limitation upon the power of the legislature to provide for their appointment by the state authorities, or otherwise.[3]

(7) For purposes of general legislation, the classification of cities and villages according to population is proper.[4]

(8) The principle of classification must be a reasonable one. The presence in a city or village of a college or university is just ground for classification.[5]

(9) Classification according to population may be proper, although at the time only one city is included in a given grade, if other cities may come into the same grade by growth in population, and municipal action.[6]

---

reason or meaning of this inhibition of the constitution." Reference is made to *State v. Cincinnati*, 20 Ohio St., 18, where on page 37, a similar dictum in regard to counties and townships is given, based on the decision in the case of *The Commissioners of Hamilton County v. Mighels*, 7 Ohio St., 109.

[1] State *v.* Davis, 23 Ohio St., 434, and State *v.* Cincinnati, *Ibid.*, 445, *supra*.

[2] State *v.* Covington, 29 Ohio St., 102, *supra*.

[3] *Ibid.* For distinction between local and governmental functions, *cf.* Cincinnati *v.* Cameron, 33 Ohio St., 336.

[4] State *v.* Brewster, 39 Ohio St., 653.

[5] Bronson *v.* Oberlin, 41 Ohio St., 112.

[6] State *v.* City of Toledo, 48 Ohio St., 112. The act considered in this case was passed on January 22, 1889 (O. L., 86 v. 7), and conferred upon cities of the third grade of the first class the power to issue bonds for natural gas works. The question of the issue was to be submitted to the voters at the municipal or the general

(10) Any act is special, no matter what its form, if it applies to only one city, and never can apply to any other without further legislative action.[1]

The fine-spun distinctions in the decisions of the court, and the seeming uncertainty of its attitude toward city legislation, was doubtless largely the result of a division of sentiment among the judges. In the case of The State *vs.* Pugh,[2] where an act was held to be unconstitutional, owing to the impossibility of any other city than Columbus ever coming under its provisions, a dissenting opinion was delivered by Judge Okey and concurred in by Judge Follett, thus pitting two judges against three. Judge Okey said: " If the question were *res integra,* by no means could it be said to be clear that this court would hold that article thirteen, section one, of the constitution, has any application to municipal corporations." But he admitted that the series of cases already decided had left that construction settled. He then reviewed the development of classification, pointing out its necessity in order to allow

election next succeeding after the passage of the act. The municipal election came in April, and the general election in November. July 1 was the date on which population was to be determined for the advancement of cities from one class to another, by the general law. Toledo was the only city in the third grade of the first class, but there were other cities with a population between 31,500 and 90,000, the limits fixed in the code for that grade. In spite of the fact that the code declared that cities thereafter advanced from the second to the first class should form the fourth grade of the latter class, the court held that cities of the second class with more than 31,500 population might have gone into the third grade, first class, on the first of July of the year when the act under consideration was passed, skipping the fourth grade mentioned in the code, as no further provision had been made for it in the way of legislation. The court did not take into consideration that a law of 1888, O. L., 85 v. 130 had provided that cities advanced from the second class into the fourth grade of the first class, should be governed by their own laws till legislation was provided for the grade into which they entered. This shows the extremity to which the court would go to uphold special legislation under the guise of classification.

[1] State *v.* Pugh, 43 Ohio St., 98, and State *v.* Mitchell, 31 Ohio St., 592, *supra.*

[2] 43 Ohio St., 98, *supra.*

legislation fitted to the varying and imperative needs of the
large cities.   In the case of The State *vs.* Brewster,[1] this same
judge had delivered the opinion of the court upholding the
classification of cities as enacted in 1878.   He had said : " The
validity of that classification has been repeatedly recognized in
this court, and the reasons for adhering to that construction
of the constitution are cogent and satisfactory."   I think too
much emphasis can hardly be placed on the influence of those
judges who, though sometimes in the minority, at other times
had the opportunity to introduce their own opinions when delivering the opinion of the court.   It would be hard to determine whether the general assembly or the court dealt in the
more subtle legal technicalities in order to allow special legislation for cities.   At a later time in the case of The State *vs.*
Wall,[2] the results of this policy had become so ridiculous and
palpably inconsistent, that the court said : " Grave doubts may
well be entertained as to the constitutionality of this method
of classifying cities for the purpose of general legislation.   But
it has received the sanction of this court in repeated decisions
heretofore made."   The discrepancy of these remarks and
Judge Okey's opinion that municipal corporations might not
be adjudged corporate bodies in the meaning of the constitution, if the question could be reopened from the beginning,
shows the opposite tendencies within the court itself.   It seems
clear that in its vacillation the court became the dupe of the
legislature.   The conservative elements secured the sanction
of the court for the system of classification, while it was yet
semi-reasonable.   But this sanction included the optional feature with reference to advancement, which afterwards operated
so cunningly in the interests of special legislation.   But the
court having set its seal to the scheme, could only regret the
caricature of a legal system which had grown up with its sanction.   It is true that no case seems to have yet been decided
involving the constitutionality of a legislative act conferring

[1] 39 Ohio St., 653, *supra.*   [2] 47 Ohio St., 499.

powers on municipal corporations of a definite population at
the last or any succeeding census.   But after straining the
possibilities to their utmost to show that some other city besides Toledo might have come under the provisions of an act
referring to cities of the first class, third grade, before the time
required for its provisions to be carried out,[1] it could not have
decided with very good grace that it would be impossible for
more than one city to ever have a population of just 6,046.

V. *General remarks.*

After what has gone before it is needless to say that the
constitution of 1851 failed to do away with special municipal
legislation.   To any one reading the convention debates there
can be no doubt that Judge Okey's " wish was father to the
thought" that municipal corporations were not included in the
section prohibiting special grants of corporate power.   From
the legal point of view the results of the Ohio policy have
been most unfortunate, introducing a habit of legal technicality
which makes legislation a mere sophistical display.   This
study has often seemed to me more appropriate for the subject
of a humorous address than for a serious discussion.[2]   But
whether we consider the course of special legislation in Ohio
humorous or disgraceful, it is necessary to keep our patience
and look into the causes.

It is often argued by the friends of special legislation that
such laws are necessary.   Granting that a great many special
laws were required during the forty years following the adop-

---

[1] State *v.* City of Toledo, 48 Ohio St., 112, *supra.*

[2] Section two of an act passed March 29, 1873, reads : " That an act entitled,
' An Act to amend section one of an act entitled an act to repeal an act entitled,
an act supplementary to an act entitled an act authorizing the appointment of
metropolitan police commissioners in cities of the first class with a population of
less than 100,000 inhabitants at the last federal census, passed April 5, 1866,
passed March 29, 1867, and to provide a police for cities of the second class,
passed April 16, 1868,' passed May 6, 1869, be and the same is hereby repealed."
O. L., 70 v. 84.

tion of the constitution of 1851, in order to allow the cities of Ohio to attain their best development, it may yet be successfully contended that the vast majority of the special laws actually passed during that period could have been easily dispensed with under a careful system of general legislation. Either local self-government is a failure, or the popularly elected authorities of villages and cities can be trusted with the power to transfer moneys from one municipal fund to another in case of need, without a special act of the legislature. If this detailed special legislation is really a necessary thing, it seems strange that the Ohio convention of 1873 and 1874, after twenty years' experience, should have recommended to the people much more stringent provisions limiting the power of the legislature than were provided in the constitution of 1851.

Perhaps we may say that the most important forces which led to the peculiar development of Ohio legislation were these two: distrust of municipal authorities in financial matters, and the desire to allow each community to do as it pleased in the management of its local affairs if it would only ask for permission. The result of the former of these forces was the very carefully defined and limited powers of borrowing money and levying taxes granted in the general municipal acts. The result of the latter force, was the varied legislation granted for the asking to particular localities according to their individual whims. Some village wanted to sink natural gas wells, a city wanted to build a railroad or car shops, or to aid manufacturing enterprises, or the people of some locality wanted two chambers in their city council, to defend them against the one chamber that these same people had elected. In laws as well as in Convention debates, we find everywhere the evidence of unlimited confidence in the people themselves and their desires, but great distrust for the local authorities elected by the people. The legislature granted the localities what they wanted, but made them ask for it.

CHAPTER VI.

THE DEVELOPMENT OF DETROIT'S CHARTER.

A CHRONOLOGICAL outline of Detroit's legislative history would give one of the best possible illustrations of the way a city government is built up bit by bit from year to year under the system of special legislation. The trouble with such a sketch is that it becomes wearisome. It is not easy to show the true course of development, and at the same time arrange the materials of charter history in any logical order. For special legislation, even when left to its natural course according to the growing desires and needs of a given locality, especially where the locality itself is going through a course of rapid development, does not readily yield itself to a scientific analysis. But when political forces also come in to change the natural course of charter evolution, the chief characteristic of special legislation becomes its lack of logical sequence. The history of Detroit is no exception to this rule. It would be very hard, indeed, to find any clear-cut and satisfactory division of Detroit history into periods, from the point of view of local government alone. But as our main object in this study is to find out something of the relations existing between the city and the state, we may take advantage of certain fairly well-marked periods in the political history of Michigan and Detroit, in their relations to each other. These periods do, as a matter of fact, correspond roughly with different tendencies in the local government.

The first period down to 1813, when Lewis Cass became Governor of Michigan Territory, may be styled the military period. Detroit was first of all a military and trading post, for the possession of which white nations fought with each other and the Indians.[1] Its civil government was incidental. The period from 1813 to 1854 is marked by the dominance of Lewis Cass and the Democratic party in Michigan. The city and the state were in political accord, and the form of local government approached the " council system." But in 1854 the triumph of the new Republican party in the state, while the city remained Democratic, opened the way for political interference in the municipal legislation and administration. About the same time the " board system" began to be introduced into the city charter. This system appeared in all parts of the country at about that time, and proved itself to be the form of city government most adapted to the demands of legislative interference in local affairs for political purposes. Hence, although it is not at all likely that the system was first introduced into the Detroit charter for political reasons, it is quite certain that its later development was intensified by its inherent adaptability to the partisan ends of legislatures unfriendly toward the politics of the city. In the year 1889, a political revolution in Detroit brought the city and the state once more into political accord ; and while this fact has not seemed to have a very marked influence on charter legislation, there has been a slight tendency to increase the powers of the mayor in accordance with the general movement throughout the country during recent years. But the most important characteristic of this last period of Detroit's history, is the strong development of the civic spirit and the increased activity of the administration under the personal leadership of Mayor Pingree.

[1] See *Historical and Scientific Sketches of Michigan*, p. 17, where Lewis Cass says, speaking of Detroit, " How numerous and diversified are the incidents, compressed within the period of its existence ! No place in the United States presents such a series of events interesting in themselves and permanently affecting, as they occurred, its progress and prosperity. Five times has its flag changed, three different sovereignties have claimed its allegiance, and since it has been held by the United States, its government has been thrice transferred ; twice it has been beseiged by the Indians, once captured in war, and once burned to the ground."

1. *The military period, 1610 to 1813.*

As early as 1610, Frenchmen from Montreal visited the present site of Detroit, but the first permanent settlement was made by Cadillac in 1701. During all of the eighteenth century Detroit remained a military post, the houses of the settlement being crowded together inside the palisades for defense from the Indians. But although the population was very small, the post was the centre for an immense fur trade, and hence of the greatest commercial importance. Upon the capture of Montreal in 1760, the whole of the northwest passed into English hands. After that time a few Englishmen came to Detroit to live, and the American immigration set in when the post was occupied in 1796 by the United States government under Jay's treaty.

In January, 1802, the settlement was incorporated as a town by the act of the governor and legislature of the Northwest Territory, which assembled at Chillicothe.[1] The officers to be chosen for the town were five trustees, a secretary, an assessor, a collector, and a marshal. Soon after, upon the creation of the State of Ohio, Detroit was transferred to Indiana Territory, of which it remained a part till 1805, when the territory of Michigan was formed. On June 11 of this year, Detroit was burned to the ground. Very soon afterwards the judges and governor of the new territory arrived, and took matters into their own hands. They were authorized by act of Congress to adopt laws from the statutes of any of the old states, and hence for the next few years all the acts of Governor Hull and Judges Woodward and Bates were excerpts from the statute-books of New York, Massachusetts, Virginia, etc. The local acts referring to the government of Detroit were taken chiefly from Maryland. On September 13, 1806, Detroit was incorporated as a city.[2] There were to be a mayor appointed

---

[1] Farmer's *History of Detroit and Michigan*, p. 133.

[2] Mich. Terr. Laws, 4 v. 3-6.

by the governor, and a city council composed of two chambers of three members each, all elected by the people. The
mayor was given an absolute veto on all laws passed by the
council, and was to appoint all city officers except the register,
who was to be named by the governor. The powers given to
the city council, their exercise being always liable to the
mayor's veto, were very extensive. The council could provide, among other things, for sanitation, police, drainage,
lighting, repair of streets and bridges, vehicle licenses, fire
companies, markets, weights and measures, and education.
They could pass all laws necessary for carrying out these
powers, and could levy and collect taxes. To illustrate the
minuteness of the enumeration of their functions, they were
authorized to fix and regulate the size of bricks to be used in
the city, to regulate the measurement of lumber, coal and
wood, to sink wells and erect pumps, and to regulate the
weight and quality of bread. This would have been local
self-government with a vengeance, except for the absolute veto
power of the mayor appointed by the governor.

But the system appears to have been a failure. The governor and judges quarreled with each other, and governed the
people in an arbitrary fashion. On February 24, 1809,[1] Gov.
Hull, in the absence of the judges, repealed the law of 1806;
but on the return of the judges an act was passed September
16, 1810,[2] repealing all laws made for Michigan prior to the
establishment of the territory in 1805, and also all laws enacted
by Governor Hull in the absence of the judges between June
2, 1807 and September 1, 1810. Hence the act of 1802 incorporating Detroit as a town was clearly repealed, and the incorporation act of 1806 was presumably revived, though it has
now been statute law in Michigan for many years that the repeal of a repealing act does not revive the original measure.[3]
But however it may have been legally, the city of Detroit had

[1] Mich. T. L.. 4 v. 83.   [2] *Ibid.*, 1 v. 900.

[3] Howell's Annotated Statutes, sec. 3.

little government except the personal government of the territorial authorities, until the new charter was granted under Governor Cass in 1815.   It is hardly necessary to mention the fact that Detroit was in the hands of the British military for about a year after its surrender by Governor Hull in August, 1812.

II. *The council period, 1813 to 1854.*

In the year 1813 Gen. Lewis Cass, a man of New England birth and training, succeeded to the governorship of the Territory of Michigan, in place of Hull, who had been disgraced by his surrender of Detroit to the British.   Governor Cass held his position until 1831, and during that period did his best to encourage the growth of local self-government among the people.[1]   After Michigan became a state in 1837, although Cass' public activity was transferred to the field of national politics, his influence in his state was almost supreme until the new Republican party came to power in 1854.   During this whole period, the state and the city being of the same political faith, Detroit legislation seems not to have been influenced by partisan motives.   The system of city government centered in the council, and the detailed changes from year to year were made in accordance with the natural growth of local needs.   During most of this period, that is, until 1847, Detroit was the seat of the State government.   At that time the capital was removed to Lansing.   Let us proceed to take up in detail the development of the city charter under these circumstances.

The Charter of 1815.   On October 24, 1815, Detroit was reincorporated as a city by the new territorial authorities.[2] The original act of 1802 was revived and amended.   The old officers were retained, namely, five trustees, secretary, assessor, collector and marshal.   All these were to be elected annually

---

[1] Howard, *Local Const. Hist. of the U. S.*, p. 154.

[2] Mich. T. L., 1 v. 534-541.

from residents by the freeholders, the householders paying an annual rental of $40.00, and such other residents as should be given the freedom of the corporation by majority vote of the electors. The board of trustees were given general powers to establish laws and ordinances for the health, safety, cleanliness, convenience and good government of the city. All laws, ordinances and regulations of the trustees were to remain in force until the next annual meeting of the electors, when they were to be submitted to vote, and if rejected by a majority of the citizens present, were to be null and void. All taxes were also to be voted by the annual meeting. The trustees could fill vacancies in elective offices, appoint subordinate officers, call special meetings of the citizens for voting taxes, and license and regulate taverns and other public houses of entertainment. The secretary of the board of trustees was required to keep a legible copy of all laws, ordinances, etc., in a book open to the public inspection. Six years later, 1821, a supervisor of roads and highways was added to the list of city officers, and the voting qualifications were amended.[1] Henceforth all free white male citizens of the United States who had lived in the city for a year and had paid taxes were to have the right of suffrage.

The Charter of 1824. By act of August 5, 1824, Detroit was granted a new charter.[2] The elective officers were to be mayor, five aldermen, marshal, supervisor, assessor, collector and three constables, chosen annually. The mayor and aldermen together were to appoint a recorder, a treasurer and a clerk. Refusal or neglect to serve in any of the elective offices might be punished by a fine of not more than $25.00. The mayor, recorder and aldermen were to constitute the common council. No business could be transacted with both mayor and recorder absent. The recorder was to be the vice-mayor of the city. Taxes were to be voted by the people on recommendation of the council, but the amount to be levied in any one year was

[1] Mich. T. L., I v. 314.   [2] *Ibid.*, 2 v. 221–230.

not to exceed one fourth of one per cent. of the assessed valuation of all real and personal property. The mayor's court
was established, to consist of any three or more members of
the common council, always including either the mayor or recorder. This court was to be a court of record, and to have
full jurisdiction in cases of offenses against the city laws or
ordinances.

Changes in the council and executive offices. The general
form of organization provided by the charter of 1824 lasted for
more than thirty years, although a new charter was granted
in 1827,[1] and numerous amendments were passed from year to
year. The council maintained its position as the central organ
of the city government. Its composition was changed in 1839,
when the city was divided into wards, each of which was required to elect two aldermen, a constable and an assessor.[2]
The mayor retained his position as presiding officer of the
council, but had no appointive power. When the Board of
Education was organized in 1842,[3] the mayor became its
president, but kept that position for only four years.[4] In 1846
he was forbidden to preside over the mayor's court except in
the absence of the recorder,[5] but the act of 1846 was repealed
a year later.[6] The recorder lost his vote in the council in
1839. During this whole period the list of elective officers
was long. By an act of 1849 the charter officers to be elected
annually on general ticket were to be: recorder, attorney,
clerk, treasurer, marshal, superintendent of water-works, phy-
sician, director of the poor, sexton, clerk for each public
market, surveyor, three inspectors of fire-wood, and two
weigh-masters.[7] In 1827 the collector had been made an appointive officer, and a definite provision had been made that
all ministerial officers should be appointed by the common

[1] Mich. T. L., 2 v. 339-354.   [2] Mich. Laws, 1839, pp. 31-35.
[3] *Ibid.*, 1842, pp. 112-116.   [4] *Ibid.*, 1846, p. 101.
[5] *Ibid.*, pp. 19-21.   [6] *Ibid.*, 1847, p. 96.
[7] *Ibid.*, 1849, pp. 32-36.

council, and be removable at pleasure.[1]   A few years later the
constables were made subject to removal by the council for
cause.[2]   Holding more than one office had been forbidden by
the charter of 1827, but this provision was repealed in 1844,
and at the same time the council was authorized to appoint a
city auditor to hold office for three years, subject to removal
only by two-thirds vote of the entire council.[3]   By act of 1849
the council's power of removal over ministerial officers was
greatly diminished, as it could henceforth be exercised only
by two-thirds vote after showing cause and giving a hearing.[4]

Elections.   In 1837 the required city residence for electors
was reduced to six months, and a board of five election inspectors was provided, to be chosen by popular vote, and to
serve at all city elections.[5]   Two years later, with the division
of the city into wards, the election inspectors were to be the
two aldermen and the assessor chosen in each particular ward.[6]
A heavy penalty was attached to "repeating."   The term of
ward residence required of electors was fixed at ten days, but
was increased to thirty in 1841.[7]

Financial affairs.   The finances of the city were not very
well managed during this early period.   In 1827 the council
was authorized to issue due bills for payment of debts, which
were to be receivable at par for taxes and other payments to
the city, and were to be transferable without endorsement.
The amount in circulation at any one time was not to exceed
$5,000.[8]   This issue by the city of fiat money was not alto-
gether successful.   The limit of issue was disregarded, and,
although the right to issue was taken away entirely in 1842,[9]
the last of the outstanding bills were not redeemed till 1871.[10]

[1] Mich. T. L., 2 v. 570–571.
[2] *Ibid.*, 3 v. 1422.
[3] Mich. Laws, 1844, p. 101.
[4] *Ibid.*, 1849, pp. 32–36.
[5] *Ibid.*, 1837, p. 199.
[6] *Ibid.*, 1839, pp. 31–35.
[7] *Ibid.*, 1841, pp. 192–201.
[8] Mich. T. L., 2 v. 570.
[9] Mich. Laws, 1842, p. 28.
[10] Farmer's *History of Detroit and Mich.*, pp. 152–155.

In 1835 the common council was authorized to make its first loan, if the consent of the citizens' meeting could be obtained.[1] The amount of the loan was to be $50,000, payable in thirty years, and bearing interest at six per cent. The annual tax limit was raised to one-half of one per cent. in 1841.[2] Beginning with 1845,[3] almost every legislature authorized a special tax levy of $15,000 or $20,000. In 1851 provision was made for a sinking fund.[4] The council was authorized to levy a special tax to cover current interest on the debt, and $5,000 in addition, which, together with all surplus saved from the general taxes, was to be appropriated to the sinking fund.

Assessments. One of the most striking evidences of the difficulty of getting a just taxable valuation of property, is to be found in the frequent changes in the method of assessment. Until 1839 assessments were made by one elected assessor, but at this time each ward was required to elect its own assessor.[5] The assessors of the wards were then to sit together as a board of equalization for the entire city after their several assessment rolls had been left open to public inspection. This plan seems to have been unsatisfactory, for in 1846 the city was divided into three districts, each comprising two wards, and the two ward assessors in each district were required to make their assessments together.[6] But two years later it was decided that one assessor should be chosen in each district and the three should make out the rolls for the entire city jointly.[7] The very next year, 1849, the old plan of assessors elected by wards was revived,[8] and in 1850 the three-district plan was tried again.[9] One assessor was to be elected in each district for a term of three years, and the assessment for the whole city was to be made as by the act of 1848. This method was not changed till 1855.

---

[1] Mich. T. L., 3 v. 1422.   [2] Mich. Laws, 1841, pp. 192–201.

[3] *Ibid.*, 1845, p. 25.   [4] *Ibid.*, 1851, p. 41.   [5] *Ibid.*, 1839, pp. 31–35.

[6] *Ibid.*, 1846, pp. 19–21.   [7] *Ibid.*, 1848, pp. 40–45.

[8] *Ibid.*, 1849, pp. 32–36.   [9] *Ibid.*, 1850, pp. 9–12.

The schools. Education was the first of the municipal functions put into the hands of a separate board. The first act
providing for common schools in Detroit was passed in 1833.[1]
A school committee was to be elected, consisting of eighteen
members, one-third of whom were to retire each year. Teach-
ers' salaries were to be paid by tuition fees, special provision
being made for indigent children. It was not until February,
1842, that free schools were established for all children between the ages of five and twenty years.[2] At that time the
city was constituted a single school district with a board of
education consisting of the mayor, recorder, and two school
inspectors, elected by each ward. Refusal to serve could be
punished by a ten dollars fine. For the support of the schools
the common council was authorized to levy a tax, the whole
amount not to exceed one dollar for every child of school age.
In 1846 the mayor ceased to be president of the board, his
place being taken by an elected member.[3] The legislature of
1847 authorized the board to borrow $5,000 with the consent
of the freeholders, but a sinking fund was provided to extin-
guish the debt within not more than twenty years.[4] It was
specifically declared by statute that the offices of member of
the board of education and member of the common council
should not be incompatible.[5]

Corporate functions. Of course it was necessary that with
the growth of the city the functions of the government shoulp
gradually expand. In the charter of 1827 the council was authorized to contract for water supply, and also to provide for the
relief of the poor. The volunteer fire service was encouraged
by exempting firemen from jury and militia duties. The firemen were to organize into companies, make their own rules,
elect officers, and hold meetings at least once a month to test
their implements. The law went on to say, " Upon any alarm

---

[1] Mich. T. L., 3 v. 1238–1242.   [2] Mich. Laws, 1842, pp. 112–116.
[3] *Ibid.*, 1846, p. 101.   [4] *Ibid.*, 1847, p. 50.   [5] *Ibid.*, 1847, p. 96.

or breaking out of any fire within said city, each member of a
fire company shall forthwith repair to the engine house, and
from thence proceed, without delay, with their fire engine
and other implements, to the place of such fire." In 1841 the
council was given full power to enact all proper ordinances
" relative to the control, regulation, protection and use of
drains and sewers."[1] It was also invested with all the powers
and functions of a township board,[2] and authorized to erect a
city jail.

The water commissioners. This gradual expansion of the
corporate functions of the city resulted in the elaboration of
the governmental machinery. The system of executive boards
did not reach its height until after 1870, but as early as 1853
an act was passed establishing the board of water commissioners.[3] This board was to consist of five members, one to retire
each year. The first commissioners were named in the act
itself,[4] but their successors were to be appointed by the common council. The board was authorized to borrow $250,000
on the credit of the city at a rate of interest not exceeding
eight per cent. Members of the board could not be interested
in any city contracts, and were allowed no compensation, but
could appoint salaried officers for the administration of the
water works. Surplus revenues were to be invested in safe
stocks, and used in paying off the bonds as they fell due.
Any deficiency in revenue was to be supplied by a special
water tax.

[1] Mich. Laws, 1841, pp. 192–201.

[2] Ever since its incorporation Detroit has had only a double system of local government. The city was never included in any township, but has had its own representatives on the county board of supervisors since the introduction of the New
York township-county system in 1827.

[3] Mich. Laws, 1853, pp. 180–187.

[4] These men had been appointed water commissioners by ordinance of the council during the previous year, so that they were really local appointees.

III. *The period of boards, 1854 to 1889.*

As already stated, a revolution in Michigan politics took place in 1854, which brought about a much sharper opposition of political interests of the city and the state than had existed before. The " board system" of city government would have been introduced, doubtless, even in the absence of these different interests, but the fact that opposite parties were in control at Detroit and Lansing could not but tend to aggravate the evils of a system, bad under almost any conditions. The direct influence of party politics on the organization of the city government by the legislature does not become apparent until 1865, when the Metropolitan Police Board was established. But the year 1855, when extensive charter amendments were passed leading up to the new charter of 1857, marks the advent of a new force in Detroit legislation. From that time on, the laws provided for the city have been more drastic, showing an increased distrust on the part of the legislature, due, no doubt, to the rapid growth of the city and the city problem, as well as to political differences.

The legislation of 1855. The first important changes under the new state regime were embodied in the act of 1855.[1] The council was authorized to appoint policemen and watchmen. It was provided that no person unable to read and write the English language should be eligible to any office except those of scavenger and chimney-sweeper. No person holding a contract for any public work was to be eligible to the council, and any contract thereafter made in which a councilman was directly or indirectly interested should be null and void. The method of assessment was changed once more. The new ward assessors were to make out their rolls without consultation, and then sit together as a board of review. But the final review and correction of the rolls was reserved for the common council. A service tax for the sewer fund was authorized,

[1] Mich. Laws, 1855, pp. 209-227.

and property could be seized and sold for a term of years in default of payment of special assessments. The creation of an almshouse department, to include an almshouse proper, houses of correction, etc., was authorized.[1] Another provision of the act of 1855 gave the council unlimited discretion to require of any officer, elected or appointed, new and additional bonds, and in case of failure, to declare the office vacant and appoint another person for the remainder of the term. Any officer could be removed by a majority vote of the members elected to the council, for such reasons as they might deem sufficient.

The Charter of 1857. Name. A new charter was granted in 1857,[2] much more elaborate than any of the preceding ones. The change in the name of the corporation shows that the American city was escaping from the traditions of the English borough. The legal title, "The Mayor, Recorder, Aldermen and Freemen of the City of Detroit," became simply the "City of Detroit."

The council and executive officers. By this charter the mayor ceased to be a member of the common council, and that body was required to elect its president from its own membership. There were to be two aldermen from each ward, as before. Outside of the council, which was still to a large extent the

---

[1] It is interesting to note the words of this provision: " Every person confined, supported, maintained or relieved in said department, whose age and health will permit, shall be employed in some useful labor, and the officers in charge thereof shall use their best endeavors to provide for all persons under their care, such labor, as on trial, shall be found to suit the capacity of the individual. It shall be the duty of the officers to keep and employ separate and apart from each other the paupers and criminals, and as far as possible to classify the latter, so that the novice in crime may not be contaminated by the evil example and converse of the more hardened and confirmed." This interesting piece of legislation was omitted from the charter of 1857. It was rather enlightened · for prison legislation in those days. The provision of which it formed a part was the legal beginning of what afterwards became the Detroit House of Correction, with Mr. Z. R. Brockway, of Elmira fame, at, its head.

[2] Mich. Laws, 1857, pp. 73–154.

central body of the administration, eight charter officers were to be chosen by the city at large, and several more by each ward. The general official term for elective officers was fixed at two years. The comptroller, who had taken the auditor's place a year or two before, was to be appointed by the council. A new executive board was established. It was to consist of three sewer commissioners appointed by the council on the mayor's nomination, to serve without compensation for terms of five years. To this new board was given the appointment of an engineer, with whose assistance a plan was to be drawn up for sewers and drains in the entire city.

Qualifications for office. Removal. Very careful provisions were made to prevent official corruption. Defaulters, of course, were ineligible to office, and the old educational qualification was continued. Members of the council were ineligible, during their terms and for one year thereafter, to any office under the charter which should be created or whose emoluments should be increased during that time. Any officer becoming interested in any contract with the city was to be removed by the common council, and be deemed guilty of corrupt malfeasance in office, and be liable to a fine not exceeding $1000 or confinement in the state's prison for not more than one year, or both fine and imprisonment, at the discretion of the court. Any person offering to bribe an officer in any way, or any officer accepting a bribe, was to be liable to the same penalties. The recorder could be impeached in the same way as any judicial officer of the state. The council might expel any one of its members or remove the comptroller or any of the elective officers (save the mayor and recorder) for corrupt or wilful malfeasance or misfeasance in office or for willful neglect of official duties, by a two-thirds vote of all the aldermen, the accused officer having been given a copy of the charges and opportunity for defense. In each case the charges, and the votes of the councilmen, were to be entered on the records. The mayor was given power to suspend or remove the marshal, street commissioners, deputy marshal, constable, overseers of highways, and officers of the police,—but he had to report the removals and his reasons to the council. That body could remove appointive officers by a majority vote of all. New official bonds might be demanded of any officer at any time by the common council, but the old special provision for declaring the office vacant in case of failure to meet the new requirements was not renewed. Thus what might have resulted in the tyranny of the council over the city officers was conditioned by the general provisions for removal.

Elections. The time of the annual charter election was changed from February to November, so as to come at the same time as the state and national elections. Each ward was constituted an election district. The inspectors of elections were to be the two aldermen together with a third person chosen by *viva voce* vote of the electors present at the opening of the polls. The voting qualifications were made to conform with those provided in the state constitution. Perjury on challenge of one's vote was made punishable by a fine of $1,000, or five years at hard labor in the state's prison, or both. " Repeating " was to be punished by a penalty of $500 fine, or three years in the state's prison, or both. No qualified voter was to be liable to arrest on civil process during election day.

The powers and duties of the council. The legislative powers of the corporation were, of course, vested in the aldermen as constituting the common council, but the mayor was given the usual veto power subject to a two thirds vote. Appointments to and removals from office and resolutions fixing salaries were not, however, subject to the mayor's veto. The council meetings were to be public, its proceedings published in a daily newspaper, and its records kept open to public inspection at reasonable times. No ordinance and no resolution imposing taxes and incurring liability could be passed at the same meeting at which they were presented, unless by unanimous consent or at a special meeting called for the purpose. No alderman could vote on any question in which he was personally interested. All others present were required to vote, and in case of tie the proposition was to be lost. All appointments to office by the council were to be made by majority vote of all aldermen elected. The president of the council was authorized to appoint such standing committees as the council should direct. Chairmen of committees and members of city boards were given power to administer oaths and summon witnesses. No officer's salary could be decreased during his incumbency, nor increased save by two-thirds vote of the council. The common council was given power—"to prohibit and prevent any riot, rout, disorderly noise, disturbance or assemblage, or the crying of any goods in the streets, or elsewhere in the city;" to prevent indecent exhibitions; to prohibit and remove nuisances ; to establish a board of health ; to prohibit and prevent the erection of dangerous buildings within a fixed limit; to suppress houses of ill-fame and assignation ; to prohibit, restrain or prevent gaming for money, and all kinds of lotteries ; to license and regulate saloons (if made lawful by the state), hotels, butcher shops, public exhibitions, bath houses, etc.; to establish a system of police; to appoint inspectors, measures, etc.; to provide for the census ; to establish almshouses, jails, etc.; to assess, levy and collect corporation taxes, etc., etc.

Revenue, finance and contracts. The revenues and moneys of the city were to be distributed among thirteen funds named in the charter, and such other funds as might be constituted by the common council. The funds named were these: (1) General fund, (2) contingent fund, (3) interest fund, (4) sinking fund, (5) fire department fund, (6) poor fund, (7) general road fund, (8) district road fund, (9) sewer fund, (10) street opening fund, (11) street paving fund, (12) public building fund, and (13) recorder's court fund. For funds numbered one, two, five, six, seven, and thirteen, the council could levy and assess gen-

eral taxes not exceeding one per cent. on the total property
valuation. Special provisions were made for the other funds,
and the city budget was to be presented to the citizens' meeting
for their approval, after the estimates for the ensuing year had
been sent in by the comptroller and revised by the council.
$30,000 a year might be levied for the sewer fund. The coun-
cil was required to levy a tax to meet current interest charges,
and also to provide between $5,000 and $10,000 a year for the
sinking fund. Special assessments could be levied for the
sewer fund, and also for the street paving fund, the amount for
the latter not to exceed $50,000 in a single year. For the
public building fund, bonds could be issued not to exceed
$300,000 in amount. The bonds had to run at least twenty
years, bear no higher than seven per cent. interest, and not be
sold below par. All contracts worth $200 or more were to be
let only to the lowest responsible bidder. The council could
not incur debt except as provided in the charter, but could
authorize the comptroller to make a temporary loan to meet
current expenses in anticipation of the annual revenue. No
warrant could be drawn on the treasury unless there was money
for the purpose named in the warrant. All warrants required
the signature of the comptroller, and the approval or authori-
zation of the common council in pursuance of law. Contracts
in which city officials were interested were to be void, as
before. At the end of each fiscal year the comptroller was
required to make a complete and detailed statement of the
financial condition of the city, to be published in two news-
papers. Such general information was to be given in addition
as would be necessary for a general understanding of the
pecuniary resources and liabilities of the city and of the condition of each fund, together with such recommendations as
he deemed advisable. Any officer or board could be required
to make estimates for the current or ensuing year, and give
accounts for any past year at any time. The mayor, comptroller and chairman of the ways and means committee were

to constitute a loan committee. The board of commissioners for the sinking fund was to be composed of the mayor, comptroller, treasurer and members of the ways and means committee.

Assessment of taxes. A new method of assessment was provided by this charter. One assessor for the entire city was to be appointed by the council on the mayor's nomination, to serve for three years and devote his whole time to the work. He was given power to appoint two assistants. The assessor, comptroller, treasurer, attorney and chairman of the ways and means committee of the council were constituted a board of review, though the final correction of the assessment rolls was left to the council.

The recorder's court. The recorder's court was established in place of the old mayor's court. In the absence of the recorder, one of the circuit judges was to preside. The court was given substantially the same privileges, powers and jurisdiction as the circuit courts had, besides having exclusive cognizance of offenses against the city ordinances. In case of persons aggrieved by the decisions of the recorder's court with reference to the city's exercise of eminent domain, an appeal was open to the state supreme court.

Charter amendments, 1859 to 1864. The charter of 1857 was granted when Detroit was in a stage of rapid development. The city had now a population of about 40,000, which had increased from 770 in 1810, 9,000 in 1840 and 21,000 in 1850. The "City of the Straits" after 150 years was really beginning to grow. The problems of municipal government were multiplying, but the whole governmental system of the city could no longer be revolutionized so easily as in the early years of its existence. There were a few important amendments passed, however, before the passage of the metropolitan police bill of 1865, when the real struggle against legislative interference and the abuses of the board system began. In 1859, the assessor was directed to separate the rural from the built-up portions of the city, and assess according to benefits enjoyed.[1] Two years later the board of review was made to consist of three resident property holders appointed for terms of three years by the council on the mayor's nomination.[2] By the same act the list of appointive officers was considerably modified, by adding the marshal, a receiver of taxes, a superintendent of the house of correction, a counselor, and, on nomination of the mayor, a fire marshal. The mayor and two other persons appointed during pleasure by the council were constituted a board of police commissioners, on whose recommendation the council was to appoint policemen and watchmen. The commissioners could remove any officer of police summarily for cause proven, and the council could dismiss any police officer at pleasure. In 1864 the terms of office of the two appointed commissioners were fixed at four years.[3]

The Metropolitan Police. February 28, 1865, marks the beginning of a new period in the legislative history of Detroit.[4] The Board of Metropolitan Police was established, to consist of four commissioners appointed from residents of Detroit by the Governor with the advice and consent of the Senate. These commissioners were to hold office for eight years, retiring one every second year, and to receive no compensation. They were to have exclusive control of the police force and the police organization, and could appoint a superintendent of police, one or more captains, sergeants, and patrolmen at salaries limited by the act. No police officer was allowed to receive fees for his services, or to hold any other office, or to accept a public nomination for any office. No police officer could be removed except for cause, and after a hearing, nor could he resign except after giving a week's notice. All vacancies in the higher ranks were to be filled by promotion· Every policeman had to be a United States citizen and a resident of Michigan for two years, able to read and write English.

---

[1] Mich. Laws, 1859, p. 1057.   [2] *Ibid.*, 1861, pp. 180–203.

[3] *Ibid.*, 1864, p. 20.   [4] *Ibid.*, 1865, pp. 99–115.

No one who had ever been convicted of a crime was eligible, and persons removed for cause could not be re-appointed. No police officer, while on duty, was allowed to enter any saloon or house of prostitution except in the actual performance of his duties. Any citizen could complain against a police officer, and cause him to be tried before the board. Members of the board could be removed by the governor in the same way as sheriffs. The expenses of the police department were to be a city charge. The board was to make an annual estimate of expenses in detail, which was to be sent in by the comptroller with his other estimates, and allowed by the council without being referred to the citizens' meeting. The books of the department were open to the inspection of the mayor or comptroller, and the council could require reasonable information at any time. Annual reports were to be made to the council. The office of city marshal was abolished, and its functions vested in the superintendent of police.

On the whole, the department of police was well organized, but the assumption of control by the state and the enforced payment of all expenses by the city without its having any voice in the administration roused a great deal of opposition. The riot of 1863 had doubtless convinced the Republican legislature that Detroit with its Democratic proclivities would not furnish adequate protection for its colored residents. There was some talk, too, that a state police organization was needed to cleanse Detroit politics. And so it is not strange that the real questions of constitutional and administrative law were somewhat obscured by the heat of party passions. Within a few years, however, the independence of the metropolitan commission was decreased. In 1867, the limit of police expenditures was fixed at $125,000 a year,[1] and in 1875 an act[2] required that the estimates of the commissioners be submitted for approval to the city Board of Estimates, a body

[1] Mich. Laws, 1867, vol. 2, pp. 265-280.

[2] Mich. Local Acts, 1875, p. 719.

consisting of two members elected from each ward and five members elected by the city at large.[1] At the special session of the Legislature in 1882, the police commissioners were given more complete control over the police force.[2] The superintendent of police, detectives, attorney, surgeon and secretary and property clerk, could be removed at pleasure.

The fire department. By act of March 26, 1867, the Fire Commission was established, to consist of four members, appointed by the council on nomination of the mayor for terms of four years.[3] Any one of the commissioners could be removed by a two-thirds vote of the common council, after having been given a chance to defend himself. A position on this board was incompatible with any political office. The estimates up to $80,000 a year were to be levied if approved by a citizens' meeting, and paid into the Detroit Fire Commission fund. The books of the commission were open at all times for the inspection of the mayor and comptroller. By an act of 1885 provision was made for pensioning firemen after twenty-five years of service.[4] In the same year a board of building inspectors was established, to consist of three mechanics or architects appointed by the board of councilmen, the newly created upper house of the city legislature.[5] These inspectors were to devote their whole time to the work and receive salaries not exceeding $1200 a year.

Parks. The problem of parks received serious attention after 1870. In 1871 a bi-partisan board of six park commissioners was established, the first members being named in the act.[6] Their successors, however, were to be appointed by the

---

[1] The board of estimates had been established in 1873 to take the place of citizens' meetings.

[2] Mich. L. A., 1882, pp. 3–5.

[3] Mich. Laws, 1867, vol. 2, pp. 931–938. The first commissioners were named in the act.

[4] Mich. L. A., 1885, pp. 470–472.   [5] *Ibid.*, pp. 552–555.

[6] Mich. Laws, 1872, vol. 2, pp. 1322–1334.

mayor and council, two retiring each year. They were authorized to investigate and advise the common council in reference
to the purchase of land for a park. The penalty attached to
the embezzlement of public funds was imprisonment in the city
House of Correction for not more than five years, or a fine of
not more than $5,000, or both. If the plans of the commis-
sioners were approved by the council, the question of issuing
bonds to carry them out was to be submitted to the citizens'
meeting. The citizens' meetings called for the purpose could
not come to a decision, and the Legislature of 1873 abolished
them altogether.[1]   To take the place of this species of referendum a board of estimates was created, to be made up of two
members from each ward and five members at large, all to hold
office for two years.   The *ex-officio* members without vote were
the president of the council, chairman of the ways and means
committee, presidents of the boards of education, police commissioners, park commissioners, and of the fire commission,
and the senior member of the board of inspectors for the house
of correction.   The board was required to decide by absolute
majority vote what estimates should be allowed for all purposes formerly submitted to the citizens' meeting. But at the
same session of the legislature the park commissioners had
been authorized to purchase a park and require the council to
issue the necessary bonds.[2]   This act was overthrown by the
courts.[3]   The matter rested until 1879, when the common
council was authorized to purchase Belle Isle for a public park,
and construct a bridge or tunnel across the Detroit river.[4]
The power to borrow money for this purpose was granted, but
the total debt of the city, not including that of the water board,
and deducting the amount in the sinking fund, was never to

[1] Mich. Laws, 1873, vol. 2, pp. 265–269, and Farmer's *History of Detroit and Michigan*, pp. 74, 75, 161.

[2] Mich. Laws, 1873, vol. 2, pp. 100–103.

[3] " Detroit Park Case," 28 Mich., 228.

[4] Mich. L. A., 1879, pp. 215–216.

exceed two per cent. of the total assessed property valuation of the city. In 1883 a new board of park commissioners was established.[1] Again, in 1889, the mayor was authorized to appoint, with the consent of the council, four electors and tax-payers to be "Commissioners of Parks and Boulevards."[2]

The board of public works. A bi-partisan board of public works, to consist of four members, the first members named in the act, and their successors to be appointed by the mayor and council for terms of eight years, was provided by the act of April 18th, 1871.[3] But the creation of the new department was bitterly opposed, by the friends of the water board, whose functions were to be transferred, and the act was declared unconstitutional by the Supreme Court.[4] In the eventfuly ear of 1873 a new act was passed creating the "Detroit board of public works," to consist of three members appointed by the council on nomination of the mayor for terms of four years.[5] $20,000 bonds were required of each. Their salaries were left to the decision of the common council, but they were expected to devote all their time to board duties. The street commissioners, overseer of highways, city surveyor, sewer commissioners, and plan and grade commissioners were superseded by the new board. An annual report covering expenditures and condition of works in each department under their control was required. A large sewer loan was authorized in 1871,[6] and the water commissioners were empowered to borrow $1,000,000, with the consent of the council, by act of 1873.[7] Provision was made for a sinking fund.

Public lighting. In 1855 the gas light company had been forbidden to increase the price of gas without the consent of the council.[8] Twenty years later the legislature authorized

---

[1] Mich. L. A., 1883, pp. 402–403.   [2] *Ibid.*, 1889, pp. 607–617.

[3] Mich. Laws. 1871, vol. 3, pp. 278–287.

[4] People *v.* Hurlbut, 24 Mich., 44.   [5] Mich. Laws, 1873, vol. 3, pp. 175–183.

[6] *Ibid.*, 1871, vol. 2, p. 1371.   [7] *Ibid.*, 1873, vol. 3, pp. 37–39.

[8] *Ibid.*, 1855. pp. 420–421.

the creation of a board of gas commissioners.[1] They were to be four in number, appointed by the mayor and council, and subject to removal on the same conditions as elective officers. With the approval of the council, existing gas plants might be purchased, and a complete establishment for supplying the city with gas might be built up. The question of raising the money by tax or loan was to be submitted to the voters of the city. The city never took advantage of the provisions of this law, although it still remains a part of the charter. The reason for this is doubtless the general substitution of electricity for gas as a public illuminant. By an act of 1887, a fund for public lighting was set apart, and the council was authorized to levy special taxes, and contract for lighting for terms of one, two or three years.[2] This provision was experimental, and led up to the construction of a city lighting plant a few years later.

The board of health. The Detroit board of health was established in 1881.[3] Three members were to be practicing physicians appointed by the board of councilmen on nomination of the mayor. The mayor, controller, and president of the board of police were to be *ex officio* members. The board was to appoint a health officer with special reference to his knowledge of chemistry, hygiene, and sanitary matters, who should give his whole time to the work. He could be removed by two-thirds vote of the board. His salary was to be fixed by the common council, not to exceed $3,000. The board of health was also given the nomination of the city physician.

The Board of Education. During this period of board government it was not strange that the financial independence of the Board of Education should be increased. In 1865 the council was required to allow the board's estimates to the

---

[1] Mich. L. A., 1875, pp. 538–541.   [2] *Ibid.*, 1887, pp. 393–395.

[3] *Ibid.*, 1881, pp. 307–308.

amount of $3.00 for every child of school age.[1] Four years later the amount of the required tax was raised to $4.00 for every child of school age.[2] The mayor and recorder were at the same time made *ex officio* members of the Board of Education, but without vote. With the approval of the citizens' meeting, a special tax not exceeding five mills on the dollar could be levied for the purpose of purchasing school lots, erecting buildings, etc., or a loan of like sum could be negotiated. By an act of 1873, the Board of Education was required to appoint a superintendent of schools for a term of three years at a maximum salary of $4,000 per year.[3] A public library building could be erected at a cost of $150,000, the money to be raised by loan or special tax approved in the regular way. The Board of Education was re-organized in 1881.[4] It was hereafter to consist of twelve school inspectors chosen, six each year, on general ticket. A district library was to be established, and the board was authorized to appoint six library commissioners. A one-fifth mill tax was to be levied annually for the support of the library. A new reorganization took place in 1889, so that one inspector was to be elected from each ward for a term of four years.[5] Women were given the franchise for the election of these inspectors.

Charities. A board of four poor commissioners was established in 1879.[6] The members were to be appointed by the council on nomination of the mayor, and were themselves authorized to appoint, with the council's consent, a secretary, a superintendent of poor, and other officers. This board was to have charge of poor relief, burial, etc. By an act of 1881 neglected families were to receive an allowance from poor commissioners,—twenty cents a day, if only a wife; thirty cents a day, if both wife and children.[7]

---

[1] Mich. Laws, 1865, p. 350.   [2] *Ibid.*, 1869, vol. 2, pp. 71–77.

[3] *Ibid.*, 1873, vol. 3, pp. 74–80.   [4] Mich. L. A., 1881, p. 100.

[5] *Ibid.*, 1889, p. 176.   [6] *Ibid.*, 1879, pp. 253–266.   [7] *Ibid.*, 1881, p. 342.

Changes in the council. The powers and organization of the common council were changed from time to time. In 1867 the council was authorized to fix the pay of its own members, not to exceed $1.50 apiece for each regular session actually attended.[1] Councilmen had already been made ineligible to any appointive city office. Now they became ineligible to the office of recorder, or any Wayne county office except that of notary public. A few years later the council was required to publish only such part of its proceedings as it deemed advisable.[2] In 1873 it was empowered to levy a special tax of $2,000 annually for the expense of public receptions, entertainments and celebrations.[3] An act of 1881 gave Detroit a bicameral legislature.[4] There had been only one chamber since the days of Governor Hull. Now an upper house was established, to be made up of twelve members elected for terms of four years on general ticket, three to retire every year. All appointments made on nomination were henceforth to be confirmed by this upper house, which was called the board of councilmen. The concurrence of both houses was of course made necessary for the passage of money bills and ordinances. All reports were to be made to the aldermen and sent by them to the upper house for concurrence. The board of estimates was abolished and its functions conferred upon the board of councilmen. The president of the councilmen was to act as vice-mayor. It was also enacted that no member of the common council should hold any state legislative office, and all were required to be freeholders.[5] Their salaries were fixed at $3.00 a day for attendance at regular sessions. In 1887 the one-chambered council was reëstablished,[6] and the salary of the aldermen was fixed at $600 a year.[7] The board of estimates was established as of old, with power to approve, disapprove, or cut down the estimates laid before it.

[1] Mich. Laws, 1867, vol. 2, pp. 1110–1115.   [2] *Ibid.*, 1871, vol. 2, p. 1231.
[3] *Ibid.*, 1873, vol. 2, pp. 1279–1283.   [4] Mich. L. A., 1881, pp. 226–228.
[5] *Ibid.*, pp. 370–377.   [6] *Ibid.*, 1887, pp. 619–629.   [7] *Ibid.*, p. 765.

The charter amendments of 1879 and 1881.   The charter had been amended in important particulars both in 1879 and in 1881.   In the former year it was provided that each officer, board or commission should have the nomination of the assistants and other officers, subject always to the approval of the council.[1]   Officers could be removed by the council on representation of the superior authority, if the charge were sustained.   The assessors were directed to assess property at its cash value.   The board of review was to consist of five resident citizens and freeholders appointed by the council.   Three of the five were to be nominated by the mayor and hold office for three years, one retiring each year.   The two others were to be aldermen, one from the eastern and one from the western district of the city, nominated by the president of the council, and holding office for one year.   In 1881 it was enacted that the city of Detroit should enjoy local legislative and administrative powers as provided by the charter, together with such implied and incidental powers as were enjoyed by municipal corporations under the state laws.[2]   The two departments, legislative and administrative, were to be kept separate, and no person or body belonging to one could exercise powers belonging to the other except as provided in the charter.   The controller[3] and the water commissioners[4] were hereafter to be appointed on nomination of the mayor.

The charter of 1883.   On June 7, 1883, a new charter was granted to Detroit.[5]   The city had increased in population under the act of 1857 from 40,000 to 140,000.   The numerous acts of intervening years had put the charter into somewhat cumbrous shape, and the new statute reduced the fundamental law of the city to more definite form.   At the same time a few amendments were introduced.   Either branch of the city leg-

---

[1] Mich. L. A., 1879, pp. 215–216.   [2] *Ibid.*, 1881, pp. 251–254.

[3] *Ibid.*, p. 324.   [4] *Ibid.*, pp. 370–377.

[5] *Ibid.*, 1883, pp. 579–646.

islature could require by resolution that any officer should report at any time. Removal of any elective officer, except the mayor and the recorder, was to be by two-thirds vote of the common council in joint session, after trial. The duties of standing committees in either house were to be prescribed by general ordinance. The special functions of the old board of estimates were no longer to be exercised by the board of councilmen. The method of assessment was again changed. A non-partisan board of three assessors nominated by the mayor was established. The common council in joint session was to sit as a board of review. Persons in possession of real estate were to be held liable for taxes, whith they might afterwards recover from the owners by action in *assumpsit*, or in withholding rent. The separate fund system was retainedby the city finances. The recorder was to be chosen for six years and receive from the state the regular salary of a circuit judge, and enough more from the city to make $4,000 a year.

Elections.—The problem of elections claimed the serious attention of the legislature during the next few years. In 1885 an act was passed to establish a board of commissioners of registration and election, to consist of four members appointed by the board of councilmen on nomination of the mayor, for terms of four years, one to retire each year.[1] The two leading political parties were each to have two members of the board. In each election district the commissioners were to appoint two electors, one of each party, who could read and write English, to be registers and inspectors of elections. This act was held to be unconstitutional by the Supreme Court.[2] A new law was passed two years later.[3] By this it was provided

[1] Mich. L. A., 1885, pp. 281–282.

[2] Attorney General *v*. The Board of Councilmen, 58 Mich. 213, *supra*. 59. The chief ground of the decision was that the requirement of the exclusive and equal representation of two political parties prescribed an unconstitutional test for holding office. The subdelegation of powers and the violation of the principle of local self-government were also urged against the act.

[3] Mich. L. A., 1887, pp. 910–913.

that five inspectors should be chosen annually in each election district. No elector could vote for more than three, and the five receiving the highest number of votes were to be chosen. No election could be held in a saloon or bar-room, or place contiguous thereto, and any one bringing intoxicating liquors to a polling-place was to be deemed guilty of a misdemeanor. In 1889 the registration laws were made much more stringent.[1]

IV. *Mayor Pingree's administration, 1889 till the present time.*

In November, 1889, Mr. Hazen S. Pingree was elected mayor of Detroit on the Republican ticket by a large majority. He has since been three times reëlected by increasing majorities. This fact alone, when we consider that Detroit has heretofore had a strongly Democratic population, would lead us to think that Mr. Pingree's administration must be marked by great personal vigor. We might also expect that the continued triumph of the Republican party in the city would bring a more liberal treatment from the state Legislature, which is nearly always Republican. As a matter of fact the results from the point of view of legislation have not been very striking. The one Democratic legislature elected in Michigan for many years back restored to Detroit in 1891 the control of the police.[2] After twenty-six years the appointment of the commissioners was transferred from the hands of the Governor to those of the Mayor. The consent of the council for the appointments was not required.

The powers of the mayor have been slightly increased during the last few years. In 1893, he was given a veto, subject to the usual two-thirds vote, over all financial resolutions of the Board of Education.[3] In this year, also, the department of law was established for the city.[4] At its head was placed the city counselor appointed by the mayor alone for a term of

[1] Mich. L. A., 1889, pp. 994–1005.   [2] *Ibid.*, 1891, pp. 936–938.

[3] *Ibid.*, 1893, pp. 1179–1181.   [4] *Ibid.*, pp. 1393–1396.

three years.   The counselor receives a salary of $5,000 and de-
votes all his time to the business of the city.   Along with the
growth in the mayor's power there has been an increased use
of referendum.   The question of free text-books, and similar
measures, after being passed by the Board of Education, must
be submitted to popular vote.[1]   The last issue of sewer bonds
was authorized to the amount of $1,000,000, with the consent
of the electors.[2]   And even the citizens' meeting was revived
to vote a levy beyond the amount of $150,000 for school
buildings.[3]

In 1893 the powers of the board of health were increased.[4]
It was given power to appoint a president, a health commissioner, a health officer, a special sanitary inspector, a food
inspector, a meat inspector, a milk inspector, a plumber and
sanitary inspectors.   These officers were to be chosen with
reference to their special fitness for their particular duties.
The plumbing, drainage and ventilators of the houses and public buildings were subjected to the regulations and approval of
the board, and plans for buildings being erected or repaired
were to be submitted to the board.   Owing to certain difficulties that arose in the spring of 1895 with reference to the
health administration, the legislature of that year gave the appointment of the Detroit board of health into the Governor's
hands.[5]   This act was certainly a step backward in the progress towards home-rule.   The board of health is now the only
municipal board appointed for Detroit by the state authorities.

While not very much has been done to make the charter a
model city constitution, a great deal has been done to awaken
civic spirit and introduce progressive administration.   In 1893
a public lighting commission was created, to consist of six
members appointed by the mayor and council.[6]   The council,

---

[1] Mich. L. A., 1891, pp. 938–939.   [2] *Ibid.*, p. 1037.

[3] *Ibid.*, pp. 1061–1064.   [4] *Ibid.*, 1893, pp. 1226–1229.

[5] *Ibid.*, 1895, not yet published.   [6] *Ibid.*, 1893, pp. 459–463.

by this act, was authorized to contract for public lighting, or with the approval of the citizens, to purchase an electric lighting plant, the first cost not to exceed $800,000, and manage the business directly. As a result of this law, the city now owns its own lighting plant, and is supplying itself with light at a much lower cost than under the former contract system. The last few years have been marked by much progress in street-paving and sewer construction. But perhaps the most important advance has been made with reference to the street-car system. After a long and determined fight with the old companies, the franchise of about forty miles of streets was recently awarded to a new company on favorable terms. Single fares are five cents, but eight tickets can be had for a quarter, good between 5.45 a. m. and 8 p. m., and six for a quarter, good during the rest of the twenty-four hours. The new franchise is to run for thirty years, when the city will have the right to purchase the plant for a consideration the amount of which is to be determined by arbitration.

The city of Detroit has to-day a population of about 250,-000. In the decade between 1880 and 1890 the number of inhabitants almost doubled. Detroit is clearly entering upon the career of a large city. There are no densely populated slum districts, and the city almost everywhere is clean and well-suited for residence. Mayor Pingree has made the city's corporate life very vigorous for the last six years. At the close of 1894 there were 215 miles of paved streets. The 147 miles of public sewers and 256 miles of laterals, being the total for the city up to that date, had been constructed at a cost of about five and a quarter millions of dollars. Belle Isle, the chief park of the city, has an area of nearly 700 acres, and there are several small parks scattered through the city.

The mayor's annual message of January 8, 1895, is full of suggestions and recommendations. He urges the necessity of bringing the departments into complete subordination to the executive. A part of the aldermen might well be elected at large. A general purchasing agent for the city should be provided, and all officers and boards be required to order their supplies through him. The mayor advocates municipal civil service reform, and the adoption of civil service examinations in the selection of jurors. A thorough system of independent audit is urged for all the departments. An increase of the bond limit to at least four per cent. of the assessed valuation is favored. The mayor favors the taxation of all property except that belonging to the city. Churches, railroads, works of art, etc., should no longer be exempt. He denounces the meter system as used by the water board, and recommends free water. The school board ought to be reorganized to consist of a small commission appointed by the mayor or elected by the people on general ticket. A new primary law should be enacted with stringent provisions to prevent any one but qualified voters of the district taking part. The revenue for re-paving streets, which now is taken entirely from the general treasury, should be replenished by a graded vehicle tax, like that in Denver, Colorado.

It is to be hoped that the present tendencies in the Detroit administration will continue. One of the things most needed, however, in order to allow the city to extend its activities at will, is a new charter based on the ideas of larger home-rule and administrative unity. At the present time the city government consists of a long list of elected and appointed officers, a common council of sixteen members, and the following thirteen boards and commissions: Estimates, Public Lighting, Police, House of Correction, Sinking Fund, Education, Library, Poor, Water, Health, Fire, Public Works and Park and Boulevard.

CHAPTER VII.

THE charter history of Cleveland, like that of Detroit, may be divided into four periods. In the case of Cleveland, these divisions are well-marked from the standpoint of governmental organization rather than from the standpoint of political relations. The first period lasted till 1836, and was the period of village organization. The city charter of 1836, which was in force until 1852, is what marks the second period. The adoption of general municipal laws in 1852 brings us to the third period, during which Cleveland was nominally under general laws, but practically governed to a very large extent by special acts. The charter of 1891, although in form a general law, was such a radical measure that it may be fairly said to have marked a new period in Cleveland's charter history. The last three periods may be roughly characterized as the periods of the council system, the board system and the mayor system respectively.

I. *Village organization.*

According to the custom of the times, a patch of the Ohio wilderness was laid out and christened " The City of Cleveland" by a surveying party sent out in 1796 by the Connecticut Land Company. But unlike many other " paper cities" of the Northwest, Cleveland came to be a real city, with people, and industries, and municipal organization. The township was organized in 1802, and in 1814 the village was incorporated.[1] The officers of the village were to be president, re-

[1] Ohio Laws, 13 v. 17-26.

corder, three trustees, treasurer, village marshal, and two assessors, all of them freeholders or householders, chosen by
electors of a year's residence. The corporate powers of the
village were vested in the first five officers, and they, always
including either the mayor or recorder, could pass by-laws
and ordinances not in conflict with national or state law. But
there was a special provision which forbade them to abuse, take
up, or sell the horses, cattle, sheep and hogs that might stray
into the village from outside owners. With these two limitations, the ordinance power was left free for all things seeming
" necessary and proper for the interest, safety, improvement
and convenience of said village." There was, of course, the
customary enumeration of powers granted to the corporation.
The amount of property to be owned could not be more than
enough to yield an annual income of $5,000, and the rate of
taxation was limited to a maximum of one per cent. The
records of the trustees' proceedings were to be open at all
times for the inspection of every elector.

This charter was not much changed for the next twenty
years. An act of 1827 regulated the slaughtering of animals
and provided for the suppression of certain nuisances.[1] In
1831 the first attack was made upon the excise problem.[2]
The board of trustees was empowered to grant a license
for vending spirituous liquors, on petition of twelve respectable
householders, the annual fee not to be less than $30.00. No
license could be granted for more than one year, nor unless
the grantee was of good moral character, and the trustees were
convinced that the license would be of public benefit. In
1834, the system of special assessments was introduced.[3] The
trustees were authorized to protect the land exposed to Lake
Erie, and assess the cost of the improvements on lots in proportion to benefits. Sewers and street improvements, except

[1] Ohio Local Acts, 25 v. 27 (vol. 25, p. 27).
[2] Ibid., 31 v. 223.   [3] Ibid., 32 v. 93, 94.

sidewalks, were to be paid for in the same way. During the next year a board of equalization was established to adjust the grievances caused by these special assessments ; and a board of three appraisers was appointed by the General Assembly.[1] This is an early instance of the appointment of local municipal officers by the central legislature.

II. *Cleveland under its first city charter, 1836 to 1852.*

The charter of 1836. The organization of the council. By act of March 6, 1836, the inhabitants of Cleveland were incorporated as a city.[2] The government was vested in a mayor and council, the latter to be composed of three members chosen from each ward, and as many aldermen as there were wards, elected on general ticket, but no two of them were to be residents of the same ward. The number of wards was fixed at three until the council should see fit to increase, alter or change them. This is certainly an extraordinary system, establishing a city council composed so curiously of local and general elements, with power to increase or to decrease its own numbers at pleasure. The combination of aldermen and councilmen in a single body suggests the influence of English municipal organization, while the requirement that one alderman shall be elected from each ward by vote of the entire city is the exact obverse of the general English system, which limits the residence of the voters but not that of the candidates.

The powers of the council. The powers of the council were enumerated at great length. The general clause reads,—"and further to have power and authority, and it is hereby made their duty, to make and publish from time to time all such laws and ordinances, as to them may seem necessary to suppress vice, provide for the safety, preserve the health, promote the prosperity, improve the order, comfort and convenience of said city and its inhabitants, and to benefit the trade and commerce thereof, as are not repugnant to the general laws of the

[1] O. L. A., 33 v. 220.   [2] *Ibid.*, 34 v. 271–284.

state." A city clerk and any other officers necessary to the interests of the city were to be appointed by the council. By a
two-thirds vote of this body the mayor might be allowed
compensation, and their own members might be paid not to
exceed $1.00 apiece for each meeting attended.

The mayor. It is worth while to quote in full the duties of
the mayor as outlined in this rather remarkable charter. " It
shall be the duty of the mayor," the law runs, " to keep the
seal of said city, sign all commissions, licenses and permits,
which may be granted by the city council ; to take care that
the laws of the state and of the city council are faithfully exe-
cuted ; to exercise a constant supervision and control over the
conduct of all subordinate officers, and to receive and examine
into all complaints against them, for neglect of duty ; to preside at the meetings of the city council when other duties shall
permit ; to recommend to said city council such measures as
he may deem expedient ; to expedite all such as shall be re-
solved upon by them ; and in general to maintain the peace
and good order, and advance the prosperity of the city ; as a
judicial officer he shall have exclusive original jurisdiction of
all cases for the violation of any ordinance of said city ; and in
criminal cases he is hereby vested with powers co-equal with
justices of the peace within the county of Cuyahoga, and shall
be entitled to like fees ; and he shall award all such process,
and issue all such writs as may be necessary to enforce the
due administration of right and justice throughout said city,
and for the lawful exercise of his jurisdiction, agreeably to the
usages and principles of law ; and when presiding at the meetings of the city council, he shall have a casting vote, when the
votes of the members are equal." The mayor, members of the
council, treasurer and marshal were all to be elected annually.

Financial provisions. This charter was remarkable also for
its financial provisions. The city council was given " power to
borrow money for the discharge and liquidation of any debt of
the city, either present or prospective, and to provide for the

redemption of any loan by them made, and the payment of the interest thereon ; and to pledge the revenues and property of the city therefor." This grant was made effective by the power to levy such rate of taxes as should be necessary for the discharge of lawful debts and the payment of current expenses. But the exercise of these powers was carefully guarded by a prescribed procedure insuring deliberation and responsibility. An ordinance for making a loan had to receive the affirmative votes of two thirds of the whole council, the yeas and nays being entered on the records, then be postponed at least two weeks, and be passed again in the same manner. The tax levy, also, was to be fixed by an absolute two-thirds majority. One assessor was to be appointed for each ward by the council, and that body was to determine the method of correction and equalization. Ordinary laws and ordinances had to be passed twice by an absolute majority vote.

The school system. The council was given the oversight of common schools, and authorized to divide each ward into school districts and appoint from each district one judicious and competent person to be a member of " The Board of Managers of Common Schools in the City of Cleveland." To this board was given the direction of the school administration, while the council was to furnish the funds. The schools were to be free to all white children more than four years old, and the property of colored persons was exempted from school taxation.

Subscriptions to railroad and plank road stocks. In 1838, a plan of subscribing to railroad companies was inaugurated, which turned out exceptionally profitable in Cleveland's case. The city was authorized to procure a loan and subscribe $200,-000 to the stock of a proposed railroad, to run in the direction of Pittsburg.[1] Five persons, named in the act, were, " by and with the consent of the city council of the said city of Cleveland, and the citizens thereof," appointed commissioners in

[1] O. L. A., 3⁶ v. 53.

trust to manage the required loan and its investment. Vacancies in their number could be filled by co-optation. The city council was required to provide funds for the payment of interest on the loan, and the principal when due. If the council refused, the commissioners could levy the necessary tax themselves. They were required to make semi-yearly reports to the council, and submit their books to inspection by it or its authorized committees. They were to be allowed compensation for their reasonable expenses. During the next thirteen years, before the constitutional prohibition of 1851,[1] four similar acts were passed, authorizing an aggregate subscription of $500,000 to the stocks of various railroads.[2] Cleveland's railroad investments seem to have been well administered, and were profitable in the long run. In 1845, a subscription of $50,000 to the capital stock of a plank road company was authorized, with the consent of the electors.[3] The county auditor was required to levy a yearly tax, for the payment of interest on the bonds, and the dividends on the stock were to be set aside as a sinking fund.

The excise problem. In 1839 the council was deprived of its power to grant retail liquor licenses, and taverns could be licensed only by the county court of common pleas; and the court was bidden to " specially take care that no tavern be licensed where the principal business contemplated is an habitual resort of the citizens for tippling ardent spirits, wine, ale or beer, or any other intoxicating liquors."[4] In 1850 a new departure was made by the creation of a board of excise, the first commissioners being named by the legislature.[5]

---

[1] Constitution of 1851, art. viii, sec. 6: "The general assembly shall never authorize any county, city, town, or township, by vote of its citizens or otherwise, to become a stockholder in any joint-stock company, corporation, or association whatever ; or to raise money for, or loan its credit to or in aid of, any such company, corporation or association."

[2] O. L. A., 44 v. 167 ; 47 v. 146; 49 v. 452, 502.

[3] *Ibid.*, 43 v. 403.   [4] *Ibid.*, 37 v. 383.   [5] *Ibid.*, 48 v. 356.

Their successors were to be appointed by the council for three-year terms, one retiring each year. The board was required to hold quarterly sessions, and " grant license to keep a tavern, porter-house, or house of entertainment to all applicants therefor, who, by the testimony of witnesses (to whom said board is hereby authorized to administer oaths), shall show to the satisfaction of the commissioners, such applicant to be of good habits, not addicted to drinking, and who would not in the opinion of said commissioners, permit or suffer any drunkenness, riotous, disorderly or licentious conduct, in his or her house, store or grocery, or on the premises occupied by him or her." All license fees and fines were to be turned into the city treasury.

Changes in the council and executive offices. By a charter amendment of 1841, the members of the council were prohibited from receiving pay, and the maximum salary any municipal officer could receive was fixed at $200.00 per year.[1] In 1847 the terms of the aldermen were extended to three years, one-third of the aldermen retiring each year.[2] There seems to have been some trouble with the city marshal, for whereas by the charter of 1836, he had been an elective officer with power to appoint his own deputies, both he and they were now to be appointed by the city council. In 1848 return was made to the old method of filling the office, and the council was given power to remove the marshal for cause after hearing his defense.[3] His salary was to be fixed at not more than $400.00, while his deputies were limited to $100.00 a year. Two years later, in 1850, Cleveland township was incorporated in the city, four wards were established subject to change by the council, and the number of councilmen elected by each ward was reduced to two.[4] In this same year the council was empowered to establish a board of health.[5] The number of its members, their official terms, compensation, and

[1] O. L. A., 37 v. 383.   [2] *Ibid.*, 45 v. 135.   [3] *Ibid.*, 46 v. 153.
[4] *Ibid.*, 48 v. 364.   [5] *Ibid.*, 48 v. 487.

to some extent their powers were left to the discretion of the
council.   In 1851 the city sexton was made an elective officer.[1]
Provision was also made for the union of Cleveland and
" Ohio city."[2]   The new territory annexed was to constitute
two new wards, thus increasing the membership of the council.

Taxation.   An unlimited taxing power was not left to the
city council long.   In 1841 five mills on the dollar was fixed
as the maximum rate.[3]   The levy determined upon was to be
certified by the mayor to the county auditor, and collected
with other taxes by the county treasurer.   In 1847 the tax
rate for general purposes was limited to two mills on the dol-
with four-fifths of a mill school tax and, and three-fourths of a
mill levy to pay debts already contracted.[4]   These levies were
to be determined between April 1 and June 1 of each year,
and within the same period the special assessments for street
improvements were to be fixed for the year.   In 1850 the tax
limit for general purposes was raised to three mills on the dollar.[5]   In the following year, certain real estate, recently annexed, was made subject to city taxes for railroad, school, road
and poor relief purposes only, until it should be divided and
sold or improved as city lots.[6]

Special assessments.   Methods of levying special assessments
have caused Ohio statesmen a good deal of anxiety.   One of
the mooted points has been the incidence of that part of the
burden of a local improvement resulting from the payment of
damages to injured individuals.   By an act of 1849 this part
of the expense in Cleveland was to be paid out of the city
treasury.[7]   In 1851 a change was made in the method of levying assessments for local improvements.[8]   On petition of at
least twelve freeholders for street improvements, the council
might provide for the payment of the expense by the petitioners, out of the city treasury, or by a discriminating tax if

[1] O. L. A., 49 v. 114.   [2] *Ibid.*, 49 v. 118.   [3] *Ibid.*, 39 v. 66.
[4] *Ibid.*, 45 v. 135.   [5] *Ibid.*, 48 v. 487.   [6] *Ibid.*, 49 v.11 4.
[7] *Ibid.*, 47 v. 204.   [8] *Ibid.*, 49 v. 114.

the petitioners represented one-third in value of the property to be taxed. Damages to individuals were to be added to the expense of the improvement.

The mayor's court. In 1841 jury trial was granted to persons tried before the mayor for violation of city ordinances.[1] Ten years later the city clerk was authorized to hold the mayor's court and was given concurrent jurisdiction with the mayor in cases of ordinance violation.[2]

III. *Cleveland under general laws, 1852 to 1891.*

We have now reached the end of avowedly special legislation for Cleveland, except in isolated acts. The new constitution, adopted in the year 1851, required the organization of cities by general laws.[3] Cleveland does not seem to have suffered very much from the evils of special legislation, although within the years immediately preceding the adoption of the new constitution there had been considerable legislative action, particularly relative to the excise problem and special assessments. But on the whole Cleveland had enjoyed a liberal and carefully-framed charter. The population of the city had increased from 1,075 in 1830, to 6,071 in 1840, and 17,034 in 1850. This was still a small population compared with the great aggregations of recent decades, but the period of rapid growth had set in, and the problems of municipal government taxed the wisdom of the legislature.

The general act of 1852. By the general act of 1852 for the organization of cities and villages in the state of Ohio, all the special acts referring to city charters proper were swept away.[4] Those special laws which had dealt with subjects local in their nature and under which important rights had become vested were not disturbed, of course. But a general organization for cities and villages according to classes was provided. Cities

---

[1] O. L. A., 39 v. 162. [2] *Ibid.*, 49 v. 114.

[3] Art. xiii, secs. 1 and 6. [4] Ohio Laws, 50 v. 223-259.

of the first class were those with more than 20,000 population,
and as Cleveland came within that category almost at once,
we need speak only of the organization and powers of cities of
the first class.

The council, its organization and powers. The aldermen of
the old regime were done away with, and the city council was
made to consist simply of the two trustees chosen from each
ward for terms of two years, half of them retiring every year.
Members could be expelled by a two-thirds vote of all. The
council was also given power to remove appointive officers by
an absolute majority vote, and elective officers by an absolute
two-thirds vote, after granting them a hearing. The passage
of by-laws and ordinances required a majority vote of all trustees after three readings on different days, unless otherwise
provided by three-fourths vote. Every ordinance was to have
a single object, expressed in its title, and ordinances amended
or revived were to be repeated in full. Trustees could not be
appointed to any municipal office during their term, except as
provided in the law, and they were forbidden to be interested
in any municipal contract.

Any improvement involving the condemnation of private
property required a two-thirds vote of all councilmen. The
same majority was required for any improvement to be paid
for by special assessment, unless petitioned for by two-thirds
of those to be assessed. Improvements and repairs of streets,
bridges and sewers could be undertaken only on recommendation of the board of city improvements.

The executive officers and boards. The mayor was required
in cities of the first class to make an annual report to the council with recommendations, and was given power to appoint the
chief of police and an equal number of watchmen from each
ward as determined by the council. The electors were to
choose for terms of two years, the mayor, city marshal, civil
engineer, fire engineer, treasurer, auditor, solicitor, police
judge and superintendent of markets. Upon the establish-

ment of water works the council was required to establish a board of three water works trustees, to hold for three years, and to be elected one each year. Three city commissioners were to be chosen in like manner, to enforce the ordinances of the city, superintend the cleaning, improving and lighting of the streets, commons, etc., and with the mayor and civil engineer to constitute the board of city improvements. The council was empowered to establish within the city or county an infirmary. Its management and the granting of out-door relief were to be placed in the charge of a board of three directors, also elected one each year. A house of refuge, a house of correction and workhouse, or a city prison, could likewise be established, and placed in charge of a board of directors. The annual election was to be held in April, and all persons resident within the city and entitled to vote for county officers were to be electors.

Taxation, revenue aad finance. The limit of taxation for general purposes was placed at five mills on the dollar, and for special funds as follows : Police fund, two mills ; fire department fund, one mill ; house of refuge, house of correction, work house and city prison, one and one-half mills ; water works, one-half mill ; schools, two mills ; city infirmary and poor relief, two mills ; sinking fund, one-half mill ; interest fund (required), two mills. Taxes could be levied uniformly on lots, platted or unplatted. A tax on dogs and other animals not on the state and county tax lists was authorized. Loans to the amount of $100,000 annually were permitted, but only in anticipation of revenue. Appropriations, when there were no funds in the treasury to pay them, were to be void.

Perhaps the worst feature of this law of 1852, in so far as it was intended to replace special legislation, was the narrow limitation of the borrowing power, and the minute regulation of the tax levy. If any particular city should need to undertake some large enterprise necessitating a loan, the legislature would have to be specially importuned for the grant of power, and this would certainly prove fatal to the spirit, if not the form, of general legislation.

Extension of the borrowing power. .The very next year after the passage of the general act of 1852, it was found necessary to extend the borrowing powers of cities. By the amending act of March 11, 1853,[1] any city not already having water works was authorized to borrow $500,000 for their construction. Running expenses were to be met by water rents, and a sinking fund was to be provided by special tax. Cities were also empowered to borrow money for the purchase of school lands and the erection of school buildings, while cities of the first class were authorized to procure a loan of $500,000 for public wharves, squares, parks or market places. In 1856,[2] and again in 1860,[3] the city councils of cities having water works were authorized to borrow money for the purpose of constructing main sewers. An act of 1879 gave to all municipal corporations the power to issue bonds for local improvements.[4] A two-thirds vote of the electors was first required, and the bonds could not be sold below par, or carry more than six per cent. interest. The authorized objects of the issue included the erection of various public buildings, the purchase of sites, construction of bridges, turnpike roads, etc., the refunding of debt, and the making of any local improvement authorized by law. Besides these general provisions, a great many special bond issues were authorized for Cleveland from year to year, for the improvement of the water works,[5] the construction of bridges,[6] elevated railroads,[7] market buildings,[8] a drainage conduit,[9] etc. In 1885, loans were authorized to meet the current expenses of the city government.[10]

---

[1] O. L., 51 v. 360–374.   [2] *Ibid.*, 53 v. 185.   [3] *Ibid.*, 57 v. 53.
[4] *Ibid.*, 76 v. 158.   [5] *Ibid.*, 69 v. 13; 79 v. 112.   [6] *Ibid.*, 69 v. 138.
[7] *Ibid.*, 80 v. 159.   [8] *Ibid.*, 81 v. 185.
[9] *Ibid.*, 82 v. 250.   [10] *Ibid.*, 82 v. 86.

Taxation and finance. In 1856, the limit of taxation, not including school, debt and special assessment levies, was placed at five mills on the dollar.[1] The tax limit was again disturbed in 1862, this time being fixed at four mills, not including an extra one-half mill for lighting.[2] An important era in Cleveland's financial administration was opened by the establishment of the sinking fund commission in this year, to which the city's railroad stocks were turned over.[3] In twenty years this fund increased from $361,377 to $2,700,000, at an expense of only $600 for management.[4] The five commissioners were named in the act, to hold their places permanently. Ordinary vacancies were to be filled by coöptation, with the consent of the council, while the court of common pleas of Cuyahoga county could remove any member for cause on complaint of the council, and appoint his successor. In the years following this act the General Assembly fixed the tax limit almost every year, usually raising the maximum aggregate or adding a special fund. By the municipal code of 1869,[5] the limit of taxes for general purposes was fixed, then the limits of the annual levy for ten special purposes were fixed, and finally the maximum aggregate levy for each of twenty-three more special purposes was determined. At the same time the limit of loans permitted in anticipation of revenue was raised to $200,000. A year later five new tax limits of annual levies for special purposes were added.[6] A limit was also fixed for the aggregate annual levy. By an act of 1883,[7] a new method of supervising taxation was adopted in the creation of a tax commission, consisting of the mayor, auditor, and three citizens appointed by the superior court of Cleveland.[8] No tax could be levied by the council, school

[1] O. L., 53 v. 214.　　　[2] *Ibid.*, 59 v. 72.　　　[3] *Ibid.*, 59 v. 126.

[4] E. M. Avery, " Cleveland in a Nutshell."

[5] O. L., 66 v. 145–286.　　　[6] *Ibid.*, 67 v. 68.　　　[7] *Ibid.*, 80 v. 124.

[8] The Superior Court of Cleveland was established in the year 1873. O. L., 70 v. 297.

board or any other city authority without the approval of this commission. The functions of this commission seem to have been chiefly legal, to see that any attempted taxation was duly authorized. In 1890, however, the tax commission was directed to appoint twenty assessors for Cleveland, equally from the two political parties which cast the highest vote at the preceding county election.[1] Public employment or office of any kind was made a bar to these appointments.

Deposits, contracts and appropriations.   By an act of 1888 a depositary commission, to be composed of the mayor, the president of the board of education, and the city solicitor, was required to receive bids from the various banks for the deposit of the public moneys.[2] A very rigid system of daily payments to the city treasurer by the several departments, daily deposits by him, daily statements by him and also by the depositary to the city auditor, and sworn monthly statements by the city auditor, was inaugurated. Two years later it was made unlawful for any officer, councilman or member of an executive board to contract or vote to contract, or to incur any expense or liability whatever, beyond the amount regularly and lawfully set apart for the particular department concerned.[3] It was to be unlawful for any officer to contract to pay any money not already in the public treasury to the credit of the department, and unappropriated. Another act passed in 1890 required the city council, by the first week of each fiscal half-year, to make "·detailed and specific appropriations for the several objects for which the city has to provide, apportioned to each month, of the moneys known to be in the treasury, or estimated to come into it during the six months next ensuing."[4] This action was to be submitted to the tax commissioners for approval, amendment or rejection. Expenditures for the next six months had to be kept within the appropriations, and balances left over at the end of the year

[1] O. L., 87 v. 138.   [2] *Ibid.*, 85 v. 197.
[3] *Ibid.*, 87 v. 96.   [4] *Ibid.*, 87 v. 342.

unexpended were to be recredited to the funds from which they were taken.

Special assessments. In the act of 1856 authorizing the construction of sewers, it was provided that special assessments for street improvements should not exceed fifty per cent. of the value of the lot on which they were levied, to be ascertained after the completion of the improvement.[1] Excess costs were to be a charge upon the general treasury. An act of 1860 authorized the council to divide the city into six main sewer districts, and levy sewer taxes in the several districts independently.[2] The general expense of any main sewer could be lessened by the levy of a special assessment equal to the estimated cost of an equal length of branch sewers. In 1865, the city was authorized to have its streets sprinkled on petition of a majority of adjacent owners, and to pay the expense by a special tax per foot front.[3] It was enacted in 1870 that special assessments should be limited to twenty-five per cent. of the taxable valuation of the property on which they were levied.[4] And no person could be compelled to pay in any one year more than one-tenth of the taxable valuation of his property for local improvements. But a year later the valuation was again allowed to be determined after the completion of the improvement.[5] An act of 1875 required that the cost of improving street intersections should be a general charge, and in addition at least one-fiftieth of the total expenses for a street improvement, not including sidewalks, was to be paid from the city treasury.[6] In 1881 an act provided that one-half the costs of repaving should be paid from a tax levied on the general property duplicate.[7]

Reports to the State Auditor. The nearest approach to state supervision over city administration, except by the Legislature,

[1] O. L., 53 v. 185.   [2] *Ibid.*, 57 v. 53.   [3] *Ibid.*, 62 v. 180.
[4] *Ibid.*, 67 v. 68.   [5] *Ibid.*, 68 v. 125.
[6] *Ibid.*, 72 v. 24.   [7] *Ibid.*, 78 v. 136.

that I have found in either Michigan or Ohio, was provided for by the Ohio law of April 5, 1856.[1]   One section provided that " the city clerk of each city of the first and second class shall, on or before the first Monday in June, report to the auditor of the state, the aggregate expenses of such city for the preceding year under the following heads: schools, police, streets, bridges, fire department, lights, poor, salaries and interest, and also the amount of the general city tax for all the preceding objects and for any others not enumerated, and the special taxes of the city for the same period, and the population of the city.   Any city clerk who shall neglect to make report as above provided, shall forfeit and pay the sum of $100, to be recovered before any court having jurisdiction of the subject matter in the name and for the use of the city."   This provision is still in force in Ohio, but does not seem to have had any very important results.

The board of revision.   By this act of April 5, 1856, it was also provided that " the mayor, the president of the council and the city attorney shall constitute a board of revision, which shall meet as often as once in every month, to review the proceedings of the council, and of all other departments of the city government, and report to the council whether any department of the city government has transcended its powers, whether any officer has neglected his duties, and also report whether any, and what retrenchments in the expenses of the city, and what improvements in any of the departments of its government can be made."   This provision was calculated to insure a careful and unified city administration, if we take for granted high character and ability in its members and the other city officers.   In 1886 an act was passed giving the board of revision full authority to prescribe to the several departments of the city government, the forms for their books, accounts, reports, etc., and to formulate and enforce a uniform system of accounting.[2]   By an act of 1887 the board of revis-

[1] O. L., 53 v. 57.   [2] *Ibid.*, 83 v. 169.

ion was authorized to spend each year a maximum of $1,000 for attorney, stenographer and incidental expenses in conducting investigations.[1] Persons refusing to testify before the board could be committed to jail for contempt.

The appointment of officers. An act of 1856 made the city clerk an appointee of the council, and also required the council to choose the civil engineer, and to designate one of the city commissioners to be acting commissioner, while the two others were to become merely advisory officers.[2] The same change was to be made in the board of infirmary directors. In 1858 the superintendent of markets became an appointee of the council,[3] but in 1863 the appointment of this officer as well as that of the civil engineer and the fire engineer was conditioned on the mayor's recommendation.[4] A board of health was provided for by general law in 1867.[5] The mayor was to be *ex officio* its president, but the six other members were made appointees of the council for terms of two years. The board of directors of the house of correction authorized soon after for Cleveland was to consist of the mayor, and four resident freeholders appointed by the council on his nomination.[6] By the provisions of the municipal code of 1869,[7] of the general officers provided for cities of the first class, seven were to be elected, four appointed by the mayor with the council's consent, and two, the clerk and the auditor, were to be chosen by the council itself. Other offices to be established by ordinances were to be filled by appointment of the mayor subject to the council's approval. No less than eleven administrative boards were provided for in the code, four of them to be elected, four appointed by the mayor and council, one appointed by the council, and two composed chiefly of *ex officio* members. By an act of the next year, the auditor, clerk, solicitor, treasurer, clerk of the police court, and civil engineer

[1] O. L., 84 v. 32.   [2] *Ibid.*, 53 v. 57.   [3] *Ibid.*, 55 v. 70.

[4] *Ibid.*, 60 v. 51.   [5] *Ibid.*, 64 v. 76.

[6] *Ibid.*, 64 v. 130.   [7] *Ibid.*, 66 v. 145–286.

were given the right to appoint the subordinates in their respective departments, subject to the council's approval.[1]   It
was also provided that a board of sewer commissioners, to be
composed of five members appointed by the mayor and council, might be established by ordinance.   In 1876 the one popularly elected member of the board of improvements was made
an appointee of the council.[2]   By the new code of 1878 the
civil engineer again became an appointee of the council.[3]   A
platting commission which had been established four years before to be appointed by the council,[4] was now to consist of
three members appointed by the mayor subject to the confirmation of the council.   An act of 1883 required that no more
than three of the five infirmary directors should be appointed
from the same political party.[5]   Three years later a bi-partisan
board of elections to consist of four members appointed by the
governor was established.[6]   This board was to appoint all of
the election judges and clerks in the various precincts of the
city.

The control of the council over the administration.   Aside
from its powers of appointment, which, as we have just seen,
were considerable, especially in the first part of this period, the
council, as the central, permanent body in the city government, was given quite a large control over the action of the
administrative officers and boards.   By the act of 1853,[7] the
water works trustees were required to report monthly and annually to the city council, which was given the right to appoint a committee to investigate the water administration once
a year or oftener.   In 1861, the board of city commissioners was
abolished, and the board of improvements was henceforth to
consist of the mayor, the civil engineer, the chairman of the
council committee on streets, and one street commissioner
elected for two years.[8]   In like manner, the chairman of the

[1] O. L., 67 v. 68.   [2] *Ibid.*, 73 v. 143.   [3] *Ibid.*, 75 v. 161–419.

[4] *Ibid.*, 71 v. 116.   [5] *Ibid.*, 80 v. 46.   [6] *Ibid.*, 83 v. 11.

[7] *Ibid.*, 51 v. 360–374.   [8] *Ibid.*, 58 v. 25.

council committee on infirmary was given a place on the board of infirmary directors, along with the superintendent of infirmary, and one director elected for two years. When the board of health was established, an annual report to the council was required, but that body could not refuse to pay the health bill.[1] Similar provisions were put in force in regard to the directors of the house of correction, authorized in 1867.[2] In the following year, the board of education,[3] which had been established in 1859, to consist of one member from each ward, was given a much more independent position than heretofore.[4] The council's approval was required only for the most important financial measures, such as the purchase of sites and the erection of school buildings. By the code of 1869,[5] the auditor, solicitor and civil engineer were given seats in the council without vote, for deliberation on questions affecting their respective departments. The action of most of the boards provided for in this code was made subject in part to the approval of the council. In 1870, the mayor was given a seat in the council without vote.[6] A law passed in 1876 forbade the council to delegate its contract power, and required a majority vote of the whole council to make contracts and adopt ordinances.[7] Contracts made in violation of these provisions were to be void as against the corporation, but binding on the contractor. In 1881, the council was required, upon the estimate of the board of improvements, to provide for the cost of the street cleaning service, which was hereafter to be done by the street commissioner, and not by contract.[8] Only in a few such cases as this was the council deprived of its financial discretion. On the whole, with the constant changing of the administrative organization, the council maintained a fair degree of control over the most important municipal affairs.

General powers of the city. The law of 1853 gave the coun-

[1] O. L., 64 v. 76.　　[2] *Ibid.*, 64 v. 130.　　[3] *Ibid.*, 56 v. 281.
[4] *Ibid.*, 65 v. 236.　　[5] *Ibid.*, 66 v. 145–286.　　[6] *Ibid.*, 67 v. 68.
[7] *Ibid.*, 73 v. 125.　　　　　　　　　　　　　　　[8] *Ibid.*, 84 v. 67.

cil an important control over the gas supply.[1]   The council
was authorized to fix the maximum charge for gas and rent
for gas meters, and appoint inspectors to certify the correctness of bills against consumers.   By a law of the following
year, the price of gas, once fixed and accepted by the gas company, could not be changed within ten years unless agreed
upon.[2]   By an act of 1857, no land could be annexed to any
municipal corporation without the consent of three-fourths of
the voters resident on the land to be annexed.[3]   In 1868 the
city was authorized to enter into an agreement with a charitable organization for the erection and management of a
hospital, to be partly supported by public funds[4]   In the code
of 1869, besides being given the customary police powers, the
municipality was authorized to construct canals, sewers, hos-
pitals, jails, market houses, water works, gas works, public
halls and school buildings; to provide parks, public cemeteries,
and free public libraries; and to establish health, fire and police
departments.   In 1875 Cleveland was authorized to establish
industrial schools for the benefit of destitute and neglected
children.[5]   A year later the board of improvements was required to divide the city into districts and contract for the
repair and cleaning of the streets, and the removal of garbage.[6]
An important law was passed in 1879 with reference to street
railways.[7]   The franchise could not be given except after advertising, and then only to the corporation or individual
which offered the lowest fares, and had secured the written
consent of the owners of a majority of the feet front along
the proposed line.   No franchise could be granted for more
than twenty years, and after the grant the council was for-

---

[1] O. L., 51 v. 360–374.   Cleveland is said to have had cheaper gas than any
other city in the United States, save Pittsburg.   See Griswold, " The Corporate
Birth and Growth of the City of Cleveland," West. Res. and N. O. Hist. Soc.,
Tract No. 62.

[2] O. L., 52 v. 30.   [3] *Ibid.*, 54 v. 85.   [4] *Ibid.*, 65 v. 83.

[5] *Ibid.,* 72 v. 211.   [6] *Ibid.*, 74 v. 103.   [7] *Ibid.*, 76 v. 156.

bidden to release the grantee from any of the obligations imposed by the agreement.

The police department. The still crude condition of police
organization was shown by an act of 1854, which authorized
the city council to provide for the election or appointment by
the mayor of a chief of police, lieutenants, and an equal number of night watchmen from the several wards, to hold for one
year.[1] Two years later the mayor was to appoint the chief of
police and assistants with the advice of the council.[2] By 1866
the question of police administration was becoming important.
The Assembly in that year provided a " metropolitan " board
for Cleveland, to be composed of the mayor, *ex-officio*, and
four members appointed by the Governor for eight-year terms,
one retiring every two years.[3] The Governor had also the
power of removal for good cause. The authorized expenses
of the board, including certain specified extras, were made a
city charge without the discretion of the council. Maximum
salaries were fixed. This system seems to have caused dis-
satisfaction, for two years after its adoption the city council
was authorized to remove police commissioners for good cause
by a three-fourths vote of all, and was required to divide the
city immediately into four districts in each of which a commissioner should be chosen at the next election.[4] Meanwhile all
the powers of the metropolitan board were vested in the mayor.
In 1876 the functions of the health board were transferred to
the police commissioners,[5] but a separate board of health was
again established in 1880.[6]

The fire department. An act of 1865 required the mayor,
the civil engineer and the chief fire engineer to examine halls,
churches, theaters, etc., and to give certificates showing these
structures to have abundant means of ingress and egress in
case of danger or alarm.[7] In the year 1874 a board of five

[1] O. L., 52 v. 47.   [2] *Ibid.*, 53 v. 57.   [3] *Ibid.*, 63 v. 104.

[4] *Ibid.*, 65 v. 45.   [5] *Ibid.*, 73 v. 47.

[6] *Ibid.*, 77 v. 89.   [7] *Ibid.*, 62 v. 139.

fire commissioners was established, to consist of the mayor as president, the chairman of the council committee on fire and water, and three resident freeholders appointed by the mayor and council.[1]   Contracts for more than $500 required the council's approval.   The board was to appoint the chief of the fire department and his subordinates.   But "no officer or member shall be appointed or removed on account of his religious or political opinions, nor participate in the political campaigns or conventions of any political party whatever."   This was the first of a series of attempts to put firemen and policemen beyond the influence of party politics.   The mayor was removed from the fire board in 1876, and his place was supplied by another elective member.[2]   It was deemed necessary to add to the non-partisan clause,—"but the right of each officer and member to vote at any election as he may for himself determine shall remain inviolate."   By an act of 1881, the mayor, fire marshal and assistant fire marshal were constituted a board of examiners of insecure and unsafe buildings.[3]   In 1886 the constitution of the fire commission was changed to adjust itself to the bicameral council.[4]   The mayor was to be president, and the chairmen of the committees on fire and water of the two council chambers, together with four elected members, made up the commission.   Two years later a system of building regulations was adopted, and the appointment of a building inspector and assistants by the mayor and council was authorized.[5]

The bicameral experiment.   We have already seen that in 1885 special laws were required to meet current expenses in Cleveland.   Probably, as a result of such financial mismanage-

---

[1] O. L., 71 v. 38.   [2] *Ibid.*,73 v. 76.   [3] *Ibid.,* 78 v. 76.

[4] *Ibid.*, 83 v. 184.   By an act of the same year (O. L., 83 v. 198) the chairmen of the two committees on streets were made members of the board of improvements in like manner.

[5] O. L., 85 v. 289.

ment, the General Assembly created a second chamber of the council as a check on hasty and extravagant action.[1]   As now constituted, the board of aldermen was to be composed of nine members elected by districts for two year terms, while the board of councilmen was to be composed of one member from each ward, also elected for two-year terms, but in the alternate years.   Within ten days after election each chamber was to assemble for organization and elect a president and vice-president by *vive voce* vote.   Ordinances might originate or be amended in either chamber, but had to be passed by both, and the interval of at least a week was required between the action of the two chambers on any ordinance involving expense or creating an obligation.   Each board was to meet at least twice each month, but never on the same or succeeding days, except in joint session.   An absolute majority vote of each board was required for the passage of an ordinance involving expenditure ; and the mayor was given the itemized veto-power over all important ordinances, except for special assessments, subject, as usual, to a re-passage by absolute two-thirds majorities after the lapse of at least ten days from the receipt of the veto message.   All elections of city officers and confirmations of official appointments vested in the council were to be made in joint session.   In 1887, the number of aldermen was increased to fifteen, to be elected in three districts,[2] but two years later this upper chamber of the council was abolished.[3]

Increasing powers of the mayor.   Even the new charter of Cleveland, adopted in 1891, so Gallican in its radical reconstructiveness, was preceded by legislation tending to unify the administration.   We have already noticed the increased powers given to the board of revision in 1886 and 1887 and the stringent financial measures of 1888 and 1890.   The increase of the mayor's powers is also to be noticed.   In 1856 he had been made president of the council by an act referring

[1] O. L., 82 v. 111.   [2] *Ibid.*, 84 v. 125.   [3] *Ibid.*, 86 v. 277.

to Cleveland alone.[1]   He lost this position through some of the
changes in the general law, but was given a seat in the
council without vote again in 1870.[2]   By the code of 1869[3] he
had been an *ex-officio* member of four of the executive boards,
while from time to time his powers of appointment had been
extended at the expense of the council.   In 1889 the accounts
of the city were put in charge of a comptroller, " appointed by
the mayor without the advice and consent of the council, on
the first Monday in May, 1890, and every three years thereafter."[4]   This officer could also be removed by the mayor for
incompetency.   An act of 1890 gave the mayor a veto on
orders of the police, health and fire boards, involving expenditure, subject to a four-fifths vote of the board concerned.[5]

IV. *The charter of 1891.*

The act of March 16, 1891, " to provide a more efficient
government for the cities of the second grade of the first class,"
was one of the most important and sweeping municipal acts
ever passed by an American legislature.[6]   The organization of
the city government of Cleveland was recast.   The law cov-
ering less than twenty pages, was a remarkably concise docu-
ment for an American city charter.   This was partly due to the
fact that the general powers and duties of municipalities are
prescribed in Ohio by the municipal code.   The fundamental
principles of the new charter were the separation of the executive and legislative departments and the complete unification of
the administration under the mayor.

The legislative department.   The first eleven sections of the
act refer to the legislative functions of the city government.
These are vested in a council of twenty members elected in ten
districts for terms of two years, half retiring each year.[7]

[1] O. L., 53 v. 57.   [2] *Ibid.*, 67 v. 68.   [3] *Ibid.*, 66 v. 145–286.

[4] *Ibid.*, 86 v. 366.   [5] *Ibid.*, 87 v. 343.   [6] *Ibid.*, 88 v. 105–121.

[7] The number of councilmen has since been increased to twenty-two.

Members are required to be residents of their respective districts. The council chooses its own president and vice-president, and may elect a sergeant-at-arms and a page. It also elects the city clerk. Except as specifically provided in this law, the council can exercise no power of election or appointment to any office. It must, however, establish and maintain a police force and a fire force, and provide for the appointment of a health officer and subordinates. It may also provide for appointment of officers to enforce laws in regard to markets, city scales, sealing of weights and measures, harbors and wharves, consumption of smoke and examination of stationary engineers, and such other officers in the several departments as it may deem necessary for the good government of the corporation and the full exercise of its corporate powers; and it may prescribe their duties and fix their compensation. Every ordinance, resolution or order involving expenditure, making a contract, imposing a tax or penalty, fixing water rent, or granting a franchise, must be introduced at least a week before its passage, and unless it relates to an improvement or assessment recommended by the board of control, must be submitted to the mayor for his approval or veto within ten days. He may approve or disapprove independent appropriation items. But the council by an absolute two-thirds majority may pass any measure over his veto, after at least a week's further consideration. All general ordinances and those providing for improvements to cost $500 or more must be published in at least two daily newspapers of opposite politics in the city. The council or any authorized council committee is given power to conduct investigations, subpœna witnesses, compel the production of books, commit for contempt, etc. No witness may be excused from testifying, but his testimony cannot be used in criminal proceedings against himself, except for perjury.

The executive department. The executive power of the city is vested in the mayor, heads of departments, and other officers provided for. The mayor, treasurer, police judge, prosecuting attorney of the police court, and clerk of the police court, are elected by the people as formerly. The most important change in the charter is to be found in the establishment of departments in imitation of the "Federal" government. They are six in number, namely, public works, police, fire, accounts, law, and charities and corrections. At the head of each department is a director appointed by the mayor, with the council's advice and consent, to hold until the expiration of the official term of the mayor appointing him. Each director is required to give a $20,000 bond approved by mayor and council. The salary of the mayor is $6,000; that of the director of law, $5,000; that of the other directors, $4,000 each. The mayor and directors must devote their whole time to their official duties and can hold no other public office or employment except that of notary public or militia officer. The compensation of all municipal officers must be by salary, and all fees and perquisites are to be paid into the city treasury, on penalty of forfeiture of office. All officers must be *bona fide* residents of the city and citizens of the United States. All officers and employes are forbidden to attend, or be members of or delegates to any political convention at which municipal officers are nominated, except where policemen attend on duty. In case of violation of this provision the mayor or head of the appropriate department must remove the officer or discharge the employe. All officers, clerks and employes, except as otherwise provided, are appointed by the heads of departments without the advice and consent of the council. A head of department may dismiss with written statement of reasons any officer or employe under him, except for political reasons; and provided further, that policemen and firemen must be given a hearing, if demanded, before the mayor, director of law and president of the council. Each director may prescribe rules and regulations, not inconsistent with law, for his department.

He is required to furnish the mayor or council with any information desired in relation to the affairs under him. The mayor and directors are required to co-operate in such a way as to secure the most economical purchase of supplies for all departments at uniform rates. They are given seats in the council without a vote, and they may be compelled to attend meetings. The mayor may take part in all proceedings, and each director in those affecting his department.

Duties of the mayor and directors. The law goes on to take up the duties of the mayor and the several directors in more detail. The duty of sending to the council from time to time a statement of the finances and other appropriate matters is imposed upon the chief executive. He is also given the absolute power to remove the directors and his other appointees, but the order of removal must be in writing, entered in the records of his office, and a copy must be transmitted to the council without delay. In cases of emergency, for five days, or longer if authorized by the council, the mayor may assume complete control of the police and fire forces. A private secretary is allowed him, who shall also be secretary of the board of control. The mayor is further required to call the directors together at least twice a month for consultation on city affairs, and reports may be asked for. The department of public works is in charge of a director, and includes the care, management and administration of water works, streets, public grounds and parks, including opening, improvement, repair, cleaning and lighting; public buildings and bridges, except those falling directly under the charge of some other department; sewers, drainage and dredging; surveys, maps, plans, estimates, etc.; all matters relating to or affecting highways, footways, waterways, harbors, wharves and docks; and the appointment of harbor masters and other officers authorized by the council for regulation of the navigation, trade and commerce of the corporation, in pursuance of law. The whole department is organized in three divisions, under the " superintendent of water works," the " superintendent of streets " and the " chief engineer," respectively. Under the director of police are placed the police force, police telegraphs, etc., the sealing of weights and measures, the city scales and markets, the inspection of food, and the public health functions in general. The members of the police force are to be appointed in accordance with civil service rules; and the police pension fund is placed under the charge of a board consisting of the mayor as president, the directors of police and of law, and three members of the force elected by their fellows. Under the director of the fire department are placed the fire force, its buildings, apparatus, etc.; the inspection of buildings, boilers, elevators and fire escapes; the examination, regulation and licensing of stationary engineers ; and the consumption of smoke. The fire force also is appointed under civil service rules. At the head of the department of accounts is placed a director to be known as the city auditor. He is required to keep accurate accounts of taxes, receipts, debts, appropriations, etc., and audit the accounts of each department annually or oftener. He prescribes the forms of book-keeping and reports made to him. Other detailed regulations to prevent illegal warrants and loose expenditure are in force. The director of law is known as the corporation counsel, and is the legal adviser of the city. His duty is to draw up all contracts and bonds, and indorse them, besides performing the regular duties of solicitor. Under the director of charities and corrections are ranged the work-house, the house of refuge and correction, the cemeteries, the infirmaries, and all other charitable and penal institutions established by the city.

The board of control and financial commissions. An important feature of the charter, perhaps simply a survival of past ideas, is the board of control, consisting of the mayor as president and the six directors. This board must hold at least two meetings a week, and perform the duties of the old board of improvements, commissioners of sewers, and board of revision. The old sinking fund commission, tax commission, depositary commission and annual and decennial boards of equalization are continued under the new system. But these have to do chiefly with the technical application of the system of taxation, and the performance of certain special financial duties, and do not form an essential part of the city administration.

Contracts. The only important feature of the charter still to be spoken of is the part dealing with contracts. Paved streets must be cleaned by contract. Contracts will not bind the city unless money has first been appropriated, or, if payment is to be made as the work progresses, unless a tax has been levied to meet the estimated expenditure. Contracts for more than $250 must be in writing, executed by the proper director, and approved by the council and the board of control. The usual requirements are made for receiving proposals where contracts are to be entered into for more than $500, and prohibiting a contract in which any city officer or employe is interested directly or indirectly.

Amendments to the charter. An amendment passed about a month after the original act, adopted another idea from the national government.[1] In case of the disability of the mayor, or a vacancy in his office, the heads of departments are to succeed him, with precedence as follows: Law, public works, police, fire, accounts, charities and corrections. Another act passed by the same assembly placed the valuation of property in the hands of not more than forty assessors, not more than half of them to be of the same political party, to be appointed by the county auditor and approved by the tax commission.[2]

[1] O. L., 88 v. 304.

[2] *Ibid.*, 88 v. 341. In Ohio a general re-assessment of real estate is made once in ten years by district assessors elected by the people· Township assessors are elected every year to list chattel property. The forty assessors referred to in the text perform the duties of township assessors for the forty wards of Cleveland. They do not act together in any way. Annual and decennial city and county boards of equalization are provided for by law.

The appointment of the members of the annual board of equalization was then transferred from the council to the mayor.[1]
A trace of the old system is found in the provision for the appointment of an inspector of boilers by the director of the fire
department, *subject to the approval of the council.*[2]

It is needless to follow the details of legislation further.   In
the few years since its enactment, the Cleveland charter of
1891 has maintained itself remarkably well against the on-
slaughts of piecemeal legislation.   The general assembly con-
tinues to pass about a score of acts at every session referring
to certain details of the Cleveland administration, and there is
small reason to hope that the charter will long remain ma-
terially unaltered, unless some radical reform is inaugurated in
the methods of legislation for Ohio cities.   In 1892 the school
administration of the Cleveland district was reorganized on the
plan of the city charter, the executive and legislative authorities being separated and vested in a school director and a
school council respectively.[3]   The council is composed of
seven members elected at large by the people of the city.   It
is possible that a thorough trial of this general scheme in all
city affairs may so strengthen its hold on the popular mind as
to operate successfully as a check on legislative interference.

[1] O. L., 88 v., 370.   [2] *Ibid.*, 88 v. 379.   [3] *Ibid.*, 89 v. 74.

CHAPTER VIII.

DETROIT AND CLEVELAND: A REVIEW OF THEIR MUNICIPAL. EXPERIENCE.

Organization of the council. Detroit has tried a good many things in the way of government, as we have seen. Twice the common council has consisted of two chambers, once under Governor Hull's charter of 1806, and once during the period from 1881 to 1887. The upper chamber was established in 1881 for the purpose of checking the board of aldermen in their reckless and corrupt expenditures. But the two chambers did not check each other, and in the Legislature of 1887 it was charged that the upper house had taken the lead in extravagance and corruption. The experiment under Hull was not given sufficient trial to add much to the sum of political experience, but that of 1881, where the members of the second chamber were elected by general ticket for comparatively long terms, with partial renewal every year, goes a long way to disprove the supposition that election by general ticket will insure responsibility and efficiency. Cleveland's experience has been somewhat different from that of Detroit. The council from 1836 to 1852 was composed of a single chamber, but had two kinds of members, the councillors chosen by wards and the aldermen chosen by the whole city. In 1885 Cleveland tried the bicameral council, by the establishment of an upper chamber to consist of nine members elected by districts for two-year terms. This experiment lasted four years, until 1889. In Detroit the lower chamber was known as the board of aldermen, while in Cleveland the upper chamber was given that title. In Detroit the upper chamber was given all the powers of the council in confirming appointments, and was also given the financial power formerly belonging to the citizens' meeting and later to the board of estimates. In Cleveland the election and confirmation of officers by the council were to be done in joint session. Here also both chambers were elected by popular vote, by districts, and for the same term. During most of their history, however, these two cities have had the one-chamber system, with but one class of members, usually elected, two from each ward, for two-year terms. But in Cleveland's latest charter, we find a smaller council of twenty members, elected in ten districts, each of which usually comprises four wards.[1]

Powers of the council. The functions of the council are fully as important as its form of organization. In the charter of 1806, the Detroit council was given almost unlimited powers, subject, however, to the absolute veto of the mayor. In 1815, the trustees' sphere of action was almost as large, but all ordinances had to be submitted to popular vote. In 1824, this restriction was omitted in the new charter. Until 1857, all appointive officers were chosen by the council. By the charter of that year an important power of removal was given to the council over all elected and appointed officers, save the mayor and recorder. Since that time the tendency has been to decrease the appointive powers of the council, regulate and define more minutely its general powers, and assign large parts of its administrative functions to separate commissions. But the Supreme Court has indicated in the case of Attorney General *vs.* The Common Council of Detroit,[2] that the legislature would not be permitted to deprive the council of its essential legislative functions. Probably this attitude of the court has helped to keep the common council a very important body in the Detroit government. The first city charter of Cleveland gave the council very extensive functions, backed by full financial powers. The council named all ap

---

[1] The council is now composed of twenty-two members.

[2] 29 Mich., 108, *supra.*

pointive officers.   Although its taxing and borrowing powers
were strictly limited under the general act of 1852, a pretty
full power of organizing the city administration and appointing
the officers not named in the general law, was given to it.
The tendency of the next ten years was to increase the council's power in the appointment of the various boards and
officers provided for by law.   But for the last thirty years, the
tendency has been carefully to restrict the financial powers
and gradually to take away the appointive powers of the council.
Under the last charter it is confined almost entirely to legislative functions, though its consent is still required for the appointment of the heads of departments.   In the history of
these two cities the pay of aldermen and councilmen has
ranged from nothing, or a small *per diem* allowance, to a maximum of $600 a year in Detroit at the present time.   In both
cities the council has the power of passing on all important
contracts.

The executive.   The organization and powers of the executive have gone through various forms.   The most remarkable
is the oldest, namely, the mayor appointed by the governor
and given an absolute veto over the acts of the council, in
Detroit's first city charter.   After that short-lived experiment,
and a period from 1815 to 1824 with no mayor at all, the
mayor was elected by the people, and continued to be a voting
member and president of the council until 1857 in the case of
Detroit.   In Cleveland the mayor was simply the presiding
officer of the council with no vote except in case of tie,
until 1852, when that body began to choose its own president.
In the early days of both cities the mayor was chiefly a
judicial and peace officer, though Cleveland's first charter gave
him a position as superintendent of the administration under the
direction of the council.   With the separation of the mayor
from the council came an increase in his appointive powers
and a decrease in his judicial powers.   The mayor of Detroit
also received important powers of removal by the charter

of 1857. He was given a veto over most of the acts of the
council, subject to a two-thirds vote, which he still retains.
The same is true of the mayor of Cleveland under the present
charter. The importance of the mayor has been increased in
both cities from time to time by his being made *ex-officio* member or president of certain boards, or by his being given a veto
over their proceedings. But Detroit has no unified administration, and the power of the present mayor, Mr. Pingree, is
due more to his personal qualities than to his offiicial position.
Only the city counselor and the members of the police board
are appointed by the mayor absolutely. Most of the other
heads of departments, if they may be so called, are elected by
the people, while the several boards are appointed, one or two
members at a time, by the mayor and council. In Cleveland,
on the other hand, the mayor has become the real head of the
city administration, with a cabinet of directors patterned after
the President's cabinet in the national government. One very
important feature in which Cleveland departs from the " Federal " example, however, is in giving the mayor and directors
seats in the city council for deliberation. His extensive veto
power and absolute power of removal make Cleveland's mayor
one of the most powerful and responsible officers in all our
municipal service. It should be added that the board of public works in Detroit and the directors of departments in
Cleveland are required to give all their time to their public
duties, and hence tend to become semi-professional officers.

Administrative boards. The two cities that we are considering have by no means been free from the " board system." It
is to be expected that public education shall be separated from
the ordinary municipal authorities and put under separate
management. In 1836 the council of Cleveland was authorized to appoint a school board, and in 1842 an elective board
was established in Detroit. The Cleveland school board long
ago became elective, and in 1892 was succeeded by a director
and a school council elected by the city at large, on the plan

of the city government.   In the case of Detroit the mayor was
president of the board of education at first, but was removed
in 1846.   In 1893 the financial resolutions of the board were
subjected to the mayor's veto.   The separation of school affairs from the ordinary city administration was followed by
special provisions for various other more or less independent
boards, as we have already seen.   There is no very marked
difference in the experience of the two cities on this point, except that Cleveland has at last thrown off the system for the
most part, while Detroit is as much entangled in a confusion
of authorities as ever.   Detroit, however, has had the advantage of a much fuller protection by the courts than has been
given in Ohio.   Perhaps the reaction in Cleveland has come
sooner from this fact also, that its boards have frequently been
elective, while the Detroit boards have more generally been
appointive.   Detroit still has, all told, a "baker's dozen" of
boards and commissions.   The bi-partisan principle tried ex-
tensively for the cities of Ohio and Michigan has been found
unconstitutional in the latter state.[1]

The direct vote of the people.   The direct vote of the citizens
has been a very important force in determining municipal
policy in Detroit.   From 1815 to 1824 all ordinances had to
be submitted to the people for approval or rejection, while
taxes continued to be voted by the citizens' meeting until 1873.
Since then at various times the question of issuing bonds has
been submitted to the electors, as well as certain questions belonging to the school administration.   Much less dependence
has been placed on the popular vote in Cleveland.   Occasion-
ally the question of a new loan is submitted to the electors,
but the citizens' meeting and the popular approval of ordinances
have been unknown there.   The working of local self- government in the two cities is interesting.   In Detroit, where the
people have had more power, there has been a greater struggle
against legislative interference by the establishment of centrally

[1] Attorney General *v.* The Board of Councilmen, 58 Mich., 213, *supra*.

appointed boards. There seems to have been less central interference in the case of Cleveland, and less struggle against it. This difference can probably be explained by the fact that the same political party usually controls in Cleveland and in the state of Ohio as a whole, while different parties have ruled in Detroit and the state of Michigan.

Finances. The crucial point in American city government seems to be the finances. In the charter of 1824 the maximum tax rate in Detroit was put at two and a half mills on the dollar of the valuation of real and personal property. This limit was doubled in 1841. Ten changes in the method of assessment were made during eighty years. The power to levy special assessments was first granted in 1855 for sewer purposes. Thirteen separate funds were established in 1857. Their number at the present time is legion. The tax rate had risen to 15.77 mills in 1894, on a total valuation of $209,-151,220; while the net indebtedness of the city was $3,359,-294. The limit of indebtedness is fixed by law at two per cent. of taxable valuation, while the public property now owned by the city is valued at more than $12,00c,000. Cleveland's financial history has been considerably different. As a village its tax limit was placed at one per cent., with no borrowing power. But in 1836 an unlimited taxing and borrowing power was granted, including the right to levy special assessments. In 1841, however, the general tax rate was limited to five mills. With the introduction of general legislation under the new constitution, the taxing power was strictly limited in aggregate and in detail, and the borrowing power was taken away. Since then the General Assembly has been called upon constantly to authorize special loans and tax levies. The tax valuation of all property in the city for 1893 was $126,515,990, and the tax rate was 13.45 mills. The ordinary expenditures for 1894 were almost five million dollars. The total debt of the city was, on January 1, 1895, $10,-266, 205.32, as against city property and permanent improvements valued at $33,850,264.35. Thus we see that the financial affairs of Cleveland have been carried on in a much larger way than those of Detroit. Detroit owns its own water works and public lighting plant. Cleveland owns its water works and several cemeteries. Both cities have extensive parks.[1]

Detroit and Cleveland have had in reality about an equal amount of special legislation, though that of Cleveland has been clothed in general form. In Detroit, we find under Mayor Pingree's administration a strong development of civic spirit, and a tendency to extend the functions of city government. In Cleveland, under its new charter, we find the emphasis laid on the perfection of administrative machinery, rather than on the extension of administrative functions.

[1] See " Annual Reports," City of Detroit, 1893; City of Cleveland, 1894.

CHAPTER IX.

THE ELEMENTS OF A CITY CHARTER.

It is certainly a common remark among municipal reformers of the present time that the form of charter makes little
difference, if only competent and honest officers have the control of the administration. It is true, to be sure, that government cannot rise permanently above its source. But while it
may be readily admitted that good laws cannot forestall bad
government, it is no less certain that bad laws can seriously
interfere with the work of good officers. And thanks to this
inequality of conditions, it is seen to be necessary that we have
both good laws and good officers to administer them. There is
no loop-hole through which the people can slink away and
escape responsibility for the character of government.

The first thing to be considered in discussing forms of municipal organization is the fundamental idea of what the city corporation exists for. Is the city a business corporation or a
political unit? It is hard to define the extreme views on this
question, although there has been a good deal of loose talk
about it. It is known that in ancient times Athens and other
cities were city-states. This is also true of Venice, Florence
and other cities of the Middle Ages. But in modern times,
outside of a few German free cities, the city has been the
creature of a larger state. Still, in being subordinate to the
state, not all cities have lost their real political character. The
tremendous influence of Paris as a unit on the politics of
France in modern times is well known. It may be said with
equal truth that New York city has been a political unit in
the history of American public affairs, and it has been sug-

gested to set it off by itself as one of the commonwealths of
the Union. All American cities have been recognized in law
and in fact as governmental divisions, political in their nature.
On the other hand, British and German cities seem to have
emphasized the business side of their corporate life. The custom of advertising for a chief of police[1] or a burgomaster[2] certainly points to a somewhat different conception of city governmental functions than we are acquainted with in America.
To the municipal reformer who has seen with disgust the
degradation of our city politics, and who has been taught to
look to the cities of the Old World for beautiful examples of
non-partisan municipal governments, it is not strange that the
idea of a city governed simply on business principles, without
any reference to politics, should appeal strongly. The result
has been a good deal of unsound thinking with reference to
municipal reforms. City government, like all government, is
both political and industrial, and it is hard to keep a true
equilibrium between these two characteristics. It is no easy
matter to tell just where business leaves off and politics begins
in governmental affairs. A great proportion of all the affairs
of government, whether national, commonwealth or municipal,
should be conducted on business principles, always keeping in
view the general welfare. In the city, with its paving, street
cleaning, sewerage, lighting, water supply, sanitation, parks,
street railways, public buildings, docks, housing regulations,
charities, excise administration, libraries and public schools,
police, and fire service, we see an accumulation of the so-called
business functions of government. It is not clear but that the
name business is applied quite indiscriminately to the comparatively recent fields of governmental activity. It is possible
that with the complete break-down of the military civilizations
of the old world and the establishment of permanent tribunals
for international arbitration, all government may some day

[1] Albert Shaw, "Municipal Gov't in Great Britain," p. 66.

[2] *Ibid.*, "Municipal Gov't in Continental Europe," p. 318.

turn into business. The point I wish to make is that city government is government, and to call it business and not politics, is simply to say that all government is tending to emphasize the industrial at the expense of the military functions. The essential thing is that, however you classify and name the activities of government, under a democratic system the individual citizen as a citizen has his share of responsibility for the success or failure of public affairs.

Next to this fundamental question, in discussing the forms of city organization we must take account of the size of the city, and the character and distribution of its population. An immense city like London or New York is too large an administrative unit to insure the greatest efficiency, and too large an elective unit to insure the most intelligent and careful choice of officers. The character of a city's population is important in determining the basis of suffrage and the qualifications for office. The presence of large aggregations of foreign-born persons not yet familiar with our institutions, the influx of tramps and semi-criminals, and the absence in suburban residences of a large proportion of the most thrifty members of the community, make the problem of municipal suffrage a serious one indeed. The problem of ward divisions is complicated by the mobility of the population, the general lack of neighborhood spirit, and the geographical differentiation of the population according to race, religion or wealth.

There are in the large cities of the modern world at least four more or less distinct types of governmental organization. In one the municipal council is the all-important central body, and not only makes the ordinances, but carries on the administration through its committees and appointees. The cities of Great Britain are organized on this plan. This was formerly the American plan also, but at the present time the council system has almost lost its hold on our municipal organizations. We have already seen that Detroit and Cleveland had this system in their early history. Minneapolis still

has council government, with some modifications.[1]   A second
type of municipal organization is that prevalent in the French
and German cities, where the council chooses the executive,
but has no power of removal.   The mayor and his adjuncts in
France and the burgomaster and his staff in Germany are the
real heads of the administration, and once in their positions
are quite independent of the council.   In this type of municipal organization the executive officers tend to be professional,
though this is probably truer in Germany than in France, owing to the longer official terms in the former country.   A third
type of municipal organization is that represented by Cleveland and a few other American cities at the present time.   It
is the outcome of extending the separation of powers, as
worked out in the United States national system, into local
government.   The council, in this system, is confined to legislative functions, while the mayor, elected by the people, is
given very full powers as chief executive and head of the administration.   The judicial power is vested in a separate
system of city courts, so that the division of the government
into the three sets of organs is tolerably complete.   The fourth
type of city organization is the prevalent one in the United
States, and has been called the board system.   There are so
much confusion and so little uniformity in the board system
that it hardly deserves to be called a type, but it has certain
general characteristics that appear in most cases.   Cleveland
from 1852 to 1891, and Detroit since about 1853, are fairly
good examples of this system in its more moderate form.   The
government of New York city varies from this type in the great
powers that are given to the mayor in appointing the various
boards, but as the boards exist and have their duties minutely
regulated by law, while the council has been reduced almost to
a nonentity, we cannot deny the American metropolis a place

[1] For a very interesting and able account of the Minneapolis system, see *Proceedings of Minneapolis and Cleveland Conferences for Good City Government*,
pp. 93–104.

in the general category of board-governed cities. In fact this variation of the board system in favor of the mayor's power has become almost universal in our large cities. Perhaps Denver is as good an example as still survives of the board system, where the mayor and the council both have comparatively small powers. In the true board system, the members of the several boards are elected one or two at a time by the people, or appointed by the governor of the state, or appointed by the mayor and council who have very meagre powers of removal. The board system is the outcome of a very complicated set of ideas. The doctrine of piecemeal legislation, the distrust of the local council, the belief in popular election, the theory of partial renewal, the desire for non-partisanship, the idea that deliberation is required in administrative bodies, and the greed for political spoils, all have had more or less to do with the distribution of city administrative functions among boards. There is practically nothing to be said in favor of the board system as it has been developed. All agree that substantial unity or at least harmony must be attained in municipal administration by some means or other.

The council system has a good many things in its favor, first among them being the fact that some of the best governed cities in the world have that type of organization. But this statement should not be made too sweeping, for we find that the cities of continential Europe.have a type of government differing quite radically from that of the British cities, where the council system exists in its purest form. But even if we class the governments of Berlin and Buda-Pesth with those of Glasgow and Birmingham, as opposed to the kinds of city government prevalent in America, because of the lesser importance of the council in the latter, we can find no conclusive proof that a system which works well in Old World cities will necessarily give New York or Detroit a good government. Although the rapid growth of cities is in all the western world a phenomenon of the present century, and especially of the pres-

ent half century, it is still true that American conditions are
different from European conditions. The most important
difference, probably, lies in the greater race mixtures in American cities. Foreign immigration has made every one of our
large towns a world-city, with no sense of unity in its population. There has probably been also a great difference in industrial conditions in the cities of the New World and of
the Old. Although the industrial expansion in European
cities during the last few decades has been marvelous,[1] it is
hardly possible that the opening up of the vast resources of a
new country like the United States should not be attended
with more feverishness, unsteadiness and lack of co-operation
in the centres of trade and production, than would be exper-
ienced in the older and more fully developed countries of
Europe. Under our conditions the sense of social unity and
social responsibility tends naturally to be less strong. The
individual prefers to take his chances scrambling for himself.
The result is a dearth of civic feeling, an individualism that is
death to responsible self-government in densely populated districts. Now the leading characteristic of the successful council government is precisely the unity of interest, the greater
household feeling, that American cities do not have at the
present time. In the early part of the century in the isolated
settlements of the West, with the town-meeting spirit still vigorous, with a comparatively homogeneous population, with no
system of quick communication like that we now have, there
survived something of the borough spirit, and council government was possible, as we have seen in the case of Detroit and
Cleveland. But when towns grew into cities, although there
might be a good deal of local pride in particular places, it
came to be of that unfruitful and ungenerous kind that consists in scorn rather than emulation. It seems to me that this
lack of real civic spirit is the factor which must be taken into
consideration before we argue for the council plan from the

[1] Shaw, *op. cit.*, p. 290.

experience of foreign cities.   London and Paris are exceptions to the general systems of city government in England and France.   They are too cosmopolitan to have the civic spirit required for entire self-government.   Of course, other peculiar factors enter into their problems, but on this one point we find almost all American cities like them.   Hence it seems a practical necessity to modify or abandon the council system for the present in our general city polity.

From the standpoint of the city as an industrial unit, a business corporation, if we reason in the abstract, there is much to be said in favor of council government as found in Great Britain, or of the continental system where the administration is put in the hands of permanent professional officers.   We never cease to hear the cry that city administration is business, not politics, and should be conducted on a business basis. A little closer observation will show, however, that the management of cities in the United States has been carried on in too much the same way as our great business corporations. The rings of city bosses and the rings of corporation directors have exploited the citizens and the stockholders in the interests of self-aggrandizement.   The trouble has arisen in both cases from the preoccupation in personal pursuits of the individuals exploited; it is the same old story of the lack of social spirit. Each man prefers to take his chances alone until the struggle for existence becomes too sharp to permit any longer the enormous waste arising from lack of coöperation.   It might easily be contended that the lack of sound business management is as conspicuous a failure of American life from the standpoint of social welfare as the character of our municipal governments has been.   The business principles which have brought about the amassing of so large a part of the wealth of the United States in great fortunes, certainly do not give any very great promise of bringing in the millennium if applied to city governments.   The fact is, our cities have had too much business on the corporation plan in their government.   The argu-

ment in favor of the council system from the analogy of industrial corporations is, therefore, not conclusive. The interests
of a business corporation are radically different from the interests of a city.

We may, perhaps, conclude that the council form of government is ideal in cities where there is a strong feeling that the
city is nothing but a larger household, and where municipal
administration is regarded as business and not politics. In the
United States, however, with our universal suffrage and our
democratic ideals, it is no easy matter to keep city affairs out
of the domain of politics. Our national and state governments
are based on the checks-and-balances theory, and party organization has become very deeply rooted in all grades of
government. I have little sympathy for that view of
our political fixedness which declares to be impracticable,
any governmental improvement no matter how much needed,
if only it runs counter to our century-old political traditions. One of the most hopeful things about the inflow
of foreign immigrants is that their presence among us tends
to overcome the narrow prejudices of American politics,
and opens the way for the modification of our system by the
introduction of new methods of government and administration.
Still most of our legislation is distinctly American in spirit,
and we must look for progress along the lines already laid
down in this country. The political prejudices of our people
must be reckoned with in any reformatory schemes we may
advocate. Democracy is on trial in the United States, and the
severest test of its worth has been and is presented by the
problems of city government. That type of municipal organization arising from the application of the doctrine of checks
and balances and the separation of powers in government is
firmly grounded in American public law, and is, I am inclined
to think, a necessary and perhaps desirable outgrowth of our
political ideas. As a result of the great increase in the importance of the administration in city government as opposed to

the other departments, we find a mayor under the system of the separation of powers and the concentration of responsibility a much more important officer relatively than even the President.

There is a striking analogy between the mayor-governed city of the present time and the absolute monarchies of two or three centuries ago. We are told that these absolute monarchies were founded on unorganized democratic states.[1] In the earlier development of the democratic spirit, before the people have been well-trained in self-government, the dictator system seems to be necessary. This is approximately the case now in city government. No great city population is as yet well trained in self-government on the basis of manhood suffrage. The peculiar problems of government in dense aggregations of people bring essentially enlarged spheres of activity within the domain of politics. The American tendency seems to be to regard these new problems as not essentially different in their nature from national and commonwealth problems. Although practically all municipal reformers are crying for the separation of local affairs from national and state politics, it remains true that the separation is not made, and almost at once after some so-called non-partisan uprising in the cities the people fall back within the old party lines. Democracy is still political rather than economic. Hence, if we are to have manhood suffrage, we must expect political government in the cities as well as elsewhere, at least until the masses have gained more freedom and training in industrial autonomy.[2] Political democracy, partly conscious of its own weakness, likes the one-man power. Responsibity is thus assured, and the people

[1] Burgess, " Political Science and Comparative Constitutional Law," vol. i, pp. 66, 127.

[2] Mr. Kidd, in his "Social Evolution," and other thinkers of the present day, have pointed out that while the political enfranchisement of the masses is almost complete in the western world, equality of opportunity in the social and industrial world is still an ideal to be worked out in future generations.

are less afraid of being imposed upon. As Americans we are getting to despise everything in the shape of legislative bodies.[1] Yet even in these bodies the democratic spirit crops out. In England the standing committees of the municipal councils and the one or two standing committies of the House of Commons are chosen by election, while in the United States only the national senate follows this rule. In the lower house of Congress, in both branches of the state legislatures, and in the city councils, standing committees are usually appointed by the presiding officer.[2] Thus it appears that the granting of large powers to the mayor is in line with our general political tendencies, and this policy is not likely to be soon abandoned.

If we accept for the present the general form of city organization by which the departments of government are separated, and the mayor is made the responsible political chief of the whole administration, there still remain many details to be considered. Either the council, the state legislature or a series of boards must exercise the municipal legislative powers, no matter how complete control the mayor may be given in administration. The levying of taxes, the authorizing of loans, the granting of franchises, the passing of ordnances, etc., are very important functions. The council being recognized as the sorest spot in our city polity, it becomes a serious problem how to organize this body in such a way as to insure the largest responsibility. We have seen that by Cleveland's new charter the council is composed of twenty members elected in ten districts.[3] The man who was the principal author of that charter complains that the number of councilmen is too large; three or five would do better.[4] This certainly is an extreme prop-

[1] Commons, " Proportional Representation," chap. 1.

[2] The municipal government of Chicago offers a marked exception to this rule. The mayor presides over the council, but that body elects its own committees.

[3] *Supra.* There are now twenty-two members elected in eleven districts.

[4] Hon. E. J. Blandin, *Municipal Government of Cleveland,* in the Proceedings of the Minneapolis Conference for Good City Government, pp. 112–118.

osition.   It does not seem likely that the legislative functions
of a great city can reasonably be placed in the hands of so
small a body.   It is sometimes urged in favor of a large council that the well-governed cities of Europe have large councils,
and also that it is more difficult for private corporations interested in bad government to corrupt a large council.   A question equally as important as the number of council members,
is the manner of choosing them.   Where there are two chambers of the council the tendency is to elect the upper house by
general ticket and the lower house by districts.   The objection
to the district plan in any form of government is the requirement of residence in the district for the councilman chosen by
the people of any district.   The conditions in cities are quite
different from those in the rural parts of the country, because
of the sharp local differentiations of city populations with
reference to wealth, nationality and social standing.   The difference in neighborhood feeling and acquaintance is also
marked.   In New York city, for instance, it is quite possible
for two families of the same general standing in society to live
on the same street with only a brick wall between them for
years, and not know each other's name.   In such a city a
man's neighbors are not those who live next to him, but the
people scattered through various parts of the city who meet
him at church, in business, or at the club.   Still it seems un-
just and impolitic to completely centralize the legislature of a
city with more than a quarter of a million inhabitants.   The
demands for election by general ticket and the demands for
election by district are conflicting, and can be met only by a
compromise, and perhaps a poor one.   It seems much better,
nevertheless, to elect a part of the council by general ticket
and the rest by districts, all members to sit together as a single chamber, than to separate them into two chambers according to the manner of their election.   However, if an effort is to
be made to secure local representation, ward divisions should
be permanent, and established as far as possible on the lines

of local unity.[1]   Then the number of representatives from each
ward or district should be determined from time to time by
population.   The councilmen elected on general ticket ought
to have longer terms than the others, thus giving a certain
element of permanency to the city legislature, and making the
positions in the gift of the city at large more desirable and important.

Perhaps some system of proportional representation should
be adopted in elections to the city council.   This is a much
debated question at the present time.   It does not seem to be
an easy task to find a method of proportional representation
that will work smoothly and exactly.   It is also objected that
under this system members chosen by parties would lose the
feeling of responsibility to the people of their districts, which,
under the present system, attaches to legislators as the sole
representatives of both the majority and the minority of their
constituents.   It seems probable that more conservatism is required of a legislator who must be able to command a majority of the votes of his constituents for his re-election, than of
one who may be re-elected even if the opposition comes into
the majority.   Proportional representation seems calculated to
strengthen the hold of party government by making a strong
organization necessary for every faction that desires to be represented.   Whether party government is a good or an evil is
an open question.   Most people recognize parties as a necessity.   If they are a good, then it may be well to strengthen
them by entrenching them in law.   If they are an evil, perhaps they may have to be entrenched in law in order to be
regulated.   If the objections to proportional representation
can be overcome, it may succeed in bringing us nearer to pure
democracy.   The idea of having every political sect represented in the legislature according to numbers is not strictly
in line with the established idea of republican or representative
government.   It aims, rather, at a new form of democracy, by

[1] Shaw, " Munic. Gov't in Continental Europe," pp. 32–35.

which the whole mass of the people is reproduced in miniature in the legislative body. If this is a possible and desirable thing, it can best be tried in cities where the people. are nearer to each other, and have more uniform interests.

There is room for many differences in the detailed organization of the city administration. The Cleveland system of departments, copied from the National administration, gives a good illustration of almost complete centralization. The organization by boards placed at the head of the several departments, and still under the mayor's control, might offer the advantages of deliberation in the management of parks, water works, sewers, police, etc. At any rate, to insure an efficient administration, a permanent staff of officers and clerks is required in each highly developed department. Hence the civil service should be subject to rules that will insure merit as the basis of appointment. The idea of party representation on boards and among appointees, seems to be entirely opposed to sound principles of administration. Under a party system " spoils" should certainly belong to the victors. But there is no reason for regarding the ministerial civil service as spoils in any intelligent system of party government.

While we may regard the mayor system as the best form of city organization under existing American conditions, it can hardly be accepted as the ultimate type. It is sometimes said that an all-powerful mayor can make a very good government or he can make a very bad government for the city, but at any rate he can be held responsible by the people at the next election.[1] This theory seems to be based on conditions that ought

[1] In a personal letter, dated March 5, 1896, in response to an inquiry about the working of the new Cleveland charter, Judge Blandin said :

"Your apprehension that an unified administration would tend to become a big partisan machine, was the current opinion here when the plan was proposed, and was made use of with very great effect by those who opposed its adoption. The working of the scheme has entirely disappointed their expectations, and proved the groundlessness of their fears. On the contrary, the first two mayors who were elected under the new charter were unable to secure their re-election, although

not to last. It means simply that the people are too busy to
take a continued interest in self-government, they are tired
of being imposed on by the professional politicians, and so they
will choose one man to govern them and hold him responsible
at the end of his term. Now, the science of good government
cannot be learned in one day, even by a man responsible to the
people of a great city. Under these conditions the people
choose some man to give them a good government, and the
next day after election return to their individual vocations,
thinking their duty is done. But there are in all of our cities
a class of professional politicians who do not weary of the details of the administration. If the mayor has to be taught, these
men teach him. He sees the public will through their eyes,
and becomes dependent upon them. The next mayor is likely
to be one whom the people do not choose. The mayor system
seems to be a remedy for city misgovernment adopted in im-

they gave a moderately fair administration. The politicians were unable to real-
ize their usual advantage, and blamed the administration for it. They should have
blamed the plan.

" The present administration is unlike the two former ones, highly unpopular
with the best people. The mayor has made every effort to build up a political
machine within the city government, with the result that he is to-day unpopular
with the masses of the people, so that any attempt on his part to be re-nominated
or re-elected would without doubt be overwhelmingly defeated.

" On the contrary, the school director in this city under a plan similar in principle, has been twice elected and has every prospect of being re elected this spring,
and has given an unprecedentedly good administration of school affairs. I think
I may summarize the whole situation by saying that our experience here with the
new plan has shown that a capable, honest executive would have more chance of
retaining his place than any one who sought to make the office the head of a political engine. In short, exactly the opposite of what you anticipate has been our
experience. The reason for this is that the masses of the people everywhere desire good government. Under our scheme their entire efforts can be concentrated
substantially upon the one office ; and the people, having this opportunity to choose,
usually choose aright. In the election of a multitude of officers at one time, of
course *choice* is practically out of the question; and the primaries of the dominant
parties name the public officers. I believe it to be the general opinion here that
our plan of city government defeats rather than promotes the establishment of a
powerful political machine."

patience and depending for its efficiency on the spasmodic rise of civic interest among a busy population, with little sense of unity.   If our political ideals do not come to dismal grief, the American city must in time develop a social consciousness of its own identity, and its population must gain experience in self-government.   When these two things come to pass to any great extent, it is likely that the dictatorial mayor will have to give way to a less arbitrary executive.   It seems strange that little or no attention has been given to the idea of introducing parliamentary or cabinet government into cities.   Probably this can be explained by the fact that this system is strongly political, while old-world cities and new-world reformers believe that city affairs are economic.   If, however, we go on along the lines marked out by our past experience, though perhaps faintly marked, we shall develop a fusion of business and politics in city affairs ; democracy in politics and in economics will meet in the city hall.   When questions of local financial policy, including the city ownership of street railways and electric lighting plants, really come to be recognized as political questions, we shall be a long way toward the realization of this ideal.   The parliamentary system is admirably fitted to combine administrative efficiency with political democracy.   The tenure of the executive is so precarious that the business of administration simply has to be entrusted to a corps of permanent officials.

But whatever form our future municipal charters may take, it seems tolerably certain that we shall work out the problem of democracy in the cities.   It is not important that all cities should have the same governmental organization.   The necessary thing is that they shall be allowed free self-development, while the civic spirit in them is encouraged.   This may possibly be best accomplished by granting them the right to form their own charters, as is now done in the larger cities of Missouri, California and Washington.   The relation of the city to the state, and the duty of the state to the city, will be the subject of the next chapter.

CHAPTER X.

THE two methods of dealing with the evils of special legislation for cities which we have seen tried in Michigan and Ohio, have not been successful in meeting the difficulties, although the Michigan plan has not failed so utterly in accomplishing its purpose as the Ohio plan has. The greatest obstacle to the solution of the problem lies in the genuine distrust of the political capacity of city populations felt by the rural communities. It seems that there is a real foundation for this distrust. Many thoughtful critics of the cities would attribute their incapacity for self government to their relatively large proportion of foreign-born citizens. This observation doubtless carries great weight, but there are other important factors in the problem. To be a good citizen of a large urban community requires a greater degree of self-restraint and a wider intelligence than to be a good citizen of a rural township. The functions of government are much more vital in the city. Water, light, drainage and transportation, the very essentials of every individual's every-day life, must come directly through the government or under government control. There is no need to argue further that the governmental demands upon the citizenship of cities are of a more exacting nature than those upon rural folk. On the other hand, leaving aside the difference in the race elements of population, there seems to be good reason to think that the mere fact of aggregation tends to reduce the average political capacity of citizens. Along with the opportunity for culture and wide intelligence furnished by city life, there comes an intense economic struggle which absorbs the energies of the more substantial citizens. The crowded conditions, the high cost of living, the extreme development of pleasure-giving institutions, the very noise on the pavement, all unite to destroy or prevent the habit of reflection in the people. They have no time to think. There is no solitude, except the awful solitude of the stranger in a large place. A reasonable degree of opportunity for the slow grinding process of thought is one of the essential elements in the development of political capacity. People in great cities have always tended to herd. There is a populace.

Thus it appears that democracy is really being put to an extraordinary test in our great cities. There the nature of govment is more economic and its functions more varied, and hence a greater political capacity and experience are required of the citizens. But not only the mixed race elements, but also the very conditions of city life, tend to lessen the development of these characteristics, at least for the time being. The people of the states have apparently had good reason to distrust the people of the cities in matters of self-government. Whether this distrust is short-sighted is another question. "Home-rule" is the war-cry of municipal reformers now, and has in its favor one very strong argument, not the inherent right to self-government, but the fact that only by throwing a full degree of responsibility upon the cities can their tendency to political degeneration be overcome and a true civic spirit aroused. It is a life and death question, for what is to become of democratic government when the majority of the people live in cities, unless we have taken pains to make those cities responsible self-governing communities? Of course, we cannot hope to legislate good citizenship into large masses of people off-hand. But there is no question but that the form of government, especially by its placing of responsibility, can greatly help or greatly hinder the growth of capable and honest citizenship. Still we must not be too hasty in granting complete local autonomy in local affairs; for our people are impatient of failure, and are quite ready to abandon experiments before they have been fully tried. But in the existing state of political affairs, the gravest duty devolving upon the people and the legislatures of the several commonwealths in their governmental capacity is the careful, honest and sympathetic encouragement of municipal capability and responsibility in the management of municipal affairs.

There being no centralized administration in the several commonwealths of the union, the only central control over municipalities has been that exercised by the state legislatures. This control has expressed itself chiefly in the special acts which make up so large a part of our volumes of session laws. The doctrine of the enumeration of powers has greatly limited the competence of the local authorities. Yet, in the absence of an administrative control, the very principle of local self-administration has made it necessary for the legislature to keep its powers of interference in local affairs unhampered. The system of legislative control has proven itself entirely inadequate. Some other method must be adopted. The obstacles in the way, arising from our historical development, do not make our task hopeless, for several reasons. First, we have an example of centralized administration in the national government, and so we need not go abroad to find a system for importation into the states. Second, as has already been remarked, the presence of such a large proportion of foreign citizens in our borders will render us more ready to accept the results of foreign experience in matters of detail. Third, in our own courts, notably those of Michigan, a tendency is showing itself to define more or less sharply the line of cleavage between purely local affairs and state affairs administered by local authorities. Fourth, notwithstanding the enumeration of municipal powers, which has seemed so hopelessly imbedded in American law and politics, the right has been granted to cities to form their own charters in three states of the Union.

This may be the opening wedge through whose application the idea of larger municipal powers may be adopted. Fifth, there is a very strong tendency among us to give the city a footing in constitutional law, and in spite of failures in specific methods tried, the constitution-makers have not become discouraged. Sixth, our universities are beginning to do important work in the study of municipal science and comparative constitutional and administrative law.

The position of the American city as an organ of government is peculiar. In spite of its helplessness in law, except for specific constitutional provisions in this state or that, the city is continually setting up the claim to an inherent right of self-government. In Michigan this doctrine of a higher law than the written constitution has even been recognized by the Supreme Court. The status of the city is undetermined. There are conflicting claims. As with our national government under the Articles of Confederation, law and fact do not coincide. The great problem of our future politics is to establish on a firm basis the legal relations of the city, and bring those legal relations to coincide with the demands of the city's natural position. The city is in fact a distinct unit in its public interests. It must be recognized as such in law. There have been persons willing to go so far as to advocate the erection of New York city into a separate and independent commonwealth of the Union. This suggestion will probably not soon be carried out, but if it were, the problem of city government in the United States would not be much nearer solution, for it would not be possible to make many cities into separate states. The solution will have to be worked out by the several commonwealths. It is not improbable that the city may introduce into the federal system a new category of governments.[1] With the powers of state and municipal governments

[1] In the Netherlands, the municipalities as well as the provinces are recognized in the national constitution, and their position is thus made independent of the national and provincial governments to some extent.

carefully delineated in the state constitutions, and with charters in the shape of self-framed constitutions, there is no reason why the federal experiment should not be elaborated. The great cities themselves cannot be completely centralized. The spirit of local autonomy by districts or wards will come to be more strongly developed, though unity of administration will always be more necessary for the city than for the common-wealth.

If we intend to persist in the trial of self-government, the status of the city in politics must be determined. It is hard now to discover who is to blame for city misgovernment. The habit of legislative interference is so strong that city populations are sure to be thwarted if they try to govern themselves in a responsible manner. The ultimate solution of the problem must lie in the greater centralization of general administrative functions under the state government, and the more complete localization of municipal administrative func-tions under the city government. The Ohio plan of prohib-iting special legislation altogether, is as undesirable as it is impossible. It is law on an arbitrary basis, and refuses to recognize the facts of local and special legislative needs. The Michigan plan of requiring the local choice of local officers may be in the right direction, but it certainly is incomplete. It involves the essentially illogical idea that the Commonwealth shall make the laws, but that the locality shall have some discretion about their enforcement. The experience of France and Germany proves that it is not impossible to unite state and local functions in a single officer, but in that case his responsibility is differentiated. We may at least conclude from our study that any constitutional solution of the city problem must have regard to both sets of evils now existing, those primarily affecting the state and those primarily affecting the locality. The state must be protected from the wastefulness and corruption of special legislation, but at the same time must be protected from anarchy in the enforcement of its general laws. The city must be protected from state interference in local affairs in both law-making and administration.

THE END.